Barry John's Rugby World

Barry John's Rugby World

Edited and Compiled by Barry John

Frederick Muller Limited

First published in Great Britain in 1982
by Frederick Muller Limited, London SW19 7JZ

Copyright © 1982   Barry John

British Library Cataloguing in Publication Data

John, Barry
    Barry John's world of rugby
    1. Rugby football
    I.   Title
    796.33'3   GV944.85

    ISBN 0—584—11036—7

Pictures are reproduced by the kind permission
of Colorsport (including front cover photos),
and Peter G. Bush (pp. 128—142).

CONTENTS

CONTENTS

INTRODUCTION

Interesting, lively and colourful writing about rugby and its people is as much a part of our game as is playing itself.

Many of my contemporaries have transferred their talents from the field to that of the press box and I'm sure that you will enjoy their views and witty comments as much as the magic they produced in their playing days.

Of course, 1982 was Ireland's year; for under their new captain, Ciaran Fitzgerald, and the inspired play of fly-half Ollie Campbell they won the Triple Crown for the first time since 1947. Former Irish and Lions prop Ray McLaughlin has recorded this historic feat — claiming that "the probability factor" clearly worked in their favour!

Chris Rea rejoices in one of Scotland's greatest performances when they annihilated Wales and sees a bright future for them; whilst David Duckham insists that England are good enough to repeat their success of 1981.

The saddest moment of an "up and down" season saw the premature retirement of the great and popular Bill Beaumont. John Taylor has looked at "Gentleman Bill's" career and how the present England squad is indebted to him because of his honest, no-nonsense attitude. J. T. also reminds us how Erica played a part in one of Bill's half-time speeches!

Gerald Davies looks at the Centenary Varsity game and rugby life in general at Oxbridge. Whilst D. K. Jones — the last of the true amateurs, according to Gareth Edwards — reminds us how rugby was played not so long ago.

Don Cameron prepares us for the visit of the New Zealand Maoris and David Lord reflects on the Wallaby tour of the UK and its implications.

The '81/'82 season also saw the retirement of one of Welsh rugby's greatest and most loyal servants, Derek Quinnell. Quinnell reflects on his early life and, of course, his varied and amazingly successful career. Wales, on the other hand, had another poor season and yours truly tries to spotlight some of the reasons.

I hope you enjoy this my latest book and your rugby in '82/'83.

B.J.

1
WHERE NOW WALES?

Barry John

Wales — it's now time to wake up to reality. Let's face it, our game has gone back at an alarming rate in the last two or three seasons. It needed a magnificent exhibition of fast, skilful rugby by Andy Irvine's Scots on our own patch at the National Stadium to drive that point home, and to remind people how rugby should be approached and how far Wales had dropped in the rugby ladder. In fact, the ovation given to the silky, swift skills of Rutherford, Renwick, Baird, Johnston and Irvine by the Welsh crowd still rings in my ears, as if it were an open declaration of its want.

Indeed, Scotland did Wales a favour, for they were yards faster than anything seen in Wales for years. It was as though they were all blessed with an extra gear, but of greater significance was the way they were all tuned to run and move the ball.

However, it must be remembered that it was Graham Mourie, that marvellous All Black captain, a man of great sincerity and integrity, who was moved to say, after his team had annihilated Wales in the Centenary showpiece two years ago, "At no time did Wales make us think — they were so predictable; always preoccupied in simply gaining possession and positions, with no thought as to how to use the ball."

Mourie's instant and honest observation should have

been the warning light, for it signalled the inescapable fact that Welsh rugby had completely lost its sense of direction and values — it needed to look at itself closely and quickly.

The game, in Wales, has by and large become static, set-piece orientated, with very little lateral play. Three-quarters have generally been picked for their defensive abilities rather than attack, simply because they have been required to play a subordinate supporting role to the forwards rather than be the major strike force. This attitude must, of course, change, and the Welsh Rugby Union is obviously conscious of this fact, for it has set up a committee under Vice-President Ieuan Evans which includes two former internationals, Dennis Hughes and Terry Cobner, to report on all aspects of the game.

Attitude is first and foremost. Teams must be encouraged to be creative and bring movement, mobility and pace back into the game. At the present, with a few exceptions, the play is one-paced, both in muscle and mind, and, sadly, I feel that much of this is due to deplorable standards in the basic skills.

All too often, first-class and international players fail to work the extra man clear — even when there is plenty of time and space.

Either the alignment is incorrect, or no one has recognised the need to straighten out the movement as the French do so wonderfully well.

Tony Shaw's 1981 Wallabies, for all their shortcomings and haphazard play, were perfectly drilled in creating the overlap with Mark Ella, Mike O'Connor, Andy Slack and co, masters at the sleight of hand, giving Brendon Moon a chance to exploit his speed on the flanks.

This, as far as I'm concerned, is where coaching starts.

Every player from hooker to full back should be well versed in taking and giving a pass, and this, above all, is where Welsh rugby is falling short of the required standard.

Coaches should look at and work on individuals' skills

as well as those of key team areas and combinations. Carwyn James was a master at this; even established "stars" were not above James's "clinic", and the results were amazing — ask former Welsh wing John Bevan! Whilst no one expects every club coach to possess James's incredible ability to understand, assess and evaluate each player's capability, I would certainly encourage them to adopt the same attitude — for solving one individual's fault can solve so many more.

I am a great believer in standards. Retaining standards, whatever the sport, is vital, and as for results — look at Liverpool Football Club. Liverpool, as far as I am concerned, is the epitome of how a truly great club should approach its sport. Even when winning trophies galore, they never abandoned their own standards, for that is the only recipe for continued success and for keeping one step ahead.

I believe that all top coaches in Welsh rugby should be assembled for a refresher course on attitude and for a reminder that there is something called performance as well as result. It is only through such thinking that Welsh rugby will regain its position in the eyes of the world. It's ironic that Wales is regarded as the home of coaching, that delegates from emergent countries flock to the various courses, and go home armed with a fund of knowledge, ideas and thoughts on how to approach the game — yet we do not practise what we preach.

The structure of Welsh rugby — practically all the major clubs, with the exception of London Welsh, are within a radius of 40 miles — has generally been regarded as the real strength of Welsh teams. This is still so. The intensive, competitive nature of club rugby, where every other game is a local derby, has its advantages — it certainly can show who has the temperament for the big occasion; but of late it's all been about results, and the standard of rugby has consequently suffered. A pride in performance must be restored and coaches should stress this point to individuals and to themselves. Wales, for so long the tutor, must now go back to the classroom and learn from others — there is nothing wrong in that.

I well remember 1971, when the Lions completely destroyed a powerful Wellington team 47-9 in the seventh game of the tour with a fast 15-man brand of rugby, leaving the whole country in a state of shock. Wellington were shattered, but, to their credit, they learnt, even in bitter defeat, and immediately changed their ways. Indeed, by the end of the tour the Wellington team was unrecognisable as the one that had lost to the Lions, for now it was playing Lions' rugby, and with great success. In fact, the whole New Zealand philosophy changed overnight, and it was ironic that the 1977 Lions lost the test series, when they had a decisive forward advantage over an All Black team who possessed extra pace and skill behind the scrum. This was a complete reversal of hitherto traditional roles, as was also the case with Billy Beaumont's 1980 Lions in South Africa. They were so

Brynmor Williams, Welsh captain going East! Swansea and Wales scrum-half signed for Cardiff Rugby League this year.

preoccupied with winning the forward battle that they were outwitted behind and lost the test series.

Richard Moriarty in action in the lineout against Australia.

As the laws of the game have changed, emphasis has changed; so the necessity to adapt is paramount. There is no doubt now that the negative way is out, and that speed and the development of skills are the requirements if Wales are to compete again at the top.

Perhaps the biggest curse in the Welsh game has been the reluctance to give the scrum-half quick possession, particularly from scrums. It seems that the whole of Welsh rugby has decided that it's impossible to score from set scrums. Aberavon's Mike Lewis has proved otherwise, and young Nigel Callard, the England Colts captain, demonstrated that a scrum-half can, if he picks the correct moment, burst clear from a set scrum. From

40 yards out he scored a fabulous try for Newport against the Barbarians last Easter. At international level, Irish full back Hugo MacNeill demonstrated the value of a quick release from a scrum when simply running on to a short pass from Robbie McGrath and crashing over against England — nothing outrageously clever in that.

Wales must, above all, learn from New Zealand. The All Blacks have thrown out the dreary 10-man stuff and really gone for speed — in possession, in passing and in support. Getting the ball quickly to the scrum-half, like Dave Loveridge and Mark Donaldson, is their main aim, and these two, like all New Zealand scrum-halves, possess marvellous reflexes to move the ball at lightning speed — if they can't, they're out. That's the modern way and the only way if Wales are to emerge from the wilderness.

Terry Holmes is congratulated after scoring against France.

Naturally, the national team provides the shop window, and although Wales beat Australia before Christmas, which instantly triggered off some talk of a "new era" in some quarters, I felt then that it was a little premature. Wales had shown great character in coming back from 6-13 and Richard Moriarty had an excellent debut at lock, scoring a try more reminiscent of a No. 8, a position I still feel he is more suited for. The honours definitely went to the Welsh pack and to Terry Holmes, who was, once again, heavily involved. Holmes' value to the team cannot be measured. Built like a middleweight contender, he has now found the perfect blend to accommodate and combine his vast range of talents. He

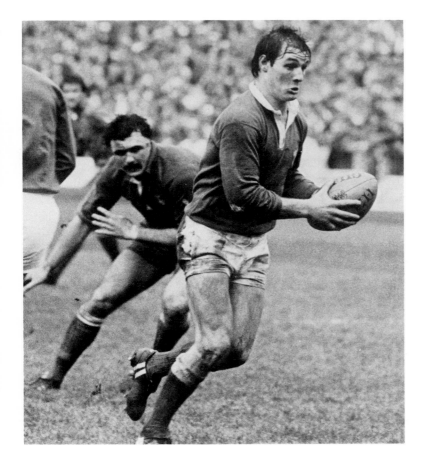

Terry Holmes breaks away.

possesses that in-built mechanism which Edwards, Going, Laidlaw and de Villiers had: knowing exactly when to run, pass or kick, and reading every situation almost to perfection.

In common with the other "greats", Holmes has that priceless ability of being able to "pull something out" when it really matters; whether it's scoring a vital try or appearing from nowhere to produce a crunching try-saving tackle. Unfortunately, shoulder injuries have restricted his appearances in the last couple of seasons and Welsh options have consequently been drastically reduced — he is that important.

Holmes' partner, Welsh captain Gareth Davies, on whom so much depends tactically, struggled from the start, and unfortunately did not really get his game together at all. Davies, like David Richards, does not seem to have overcome the shoulder injuries received in South Africa with the 1980 Lions. Confidence and that touch of arrogance, so much a part of a fly-half's armoury, were missing, and the unforced error ratio in his game was far too high.

On his day, Davies' kicking can be devastating and can destroy any team, but, alas, he can go from one extreme to the other, even in the same game. Such inconsistency does not give a team any platform on which to operate. Unfortunately, Davies' game lost all purpose and impetus, and all too often the percentage play was opted for by putting boot to ball, even when there was sufficient time to probe and explore a few possibilities.

When confidence is at a low ebb, nothing is obvious or clear in the mind. Even that innate smell for a natural opening that all fly-halves look for is picked up a split second too late, and sadly by the end of the season Davies looked a confused player. After Holmes' injury at Twickenham and the selectors decision to play Bridgend's skipper, Gerald Williams, with Davies, the perfect opportunity presented itself to relieve Davies of the added responsibility of captaining. But this was not

Gareth Davies, Welsh
captain.

taken. There is no doubt that Davies has to re-establish himself if he is to hold on to his place.

John Bevan, the former Wales and Lions fly-half, who has made Aberavon into one of Wales' most attractive and attack-conscious teams, is set to play a key part in the development of Welsh rugby. Bevan's philosophy has, to his credit, not changed since his playing days: think positively and take the game to the opposition at every given opportunity. Bevan's thinking and attitude are clear-cut, and this has worked wonders with Aberavon, who were desperately unlucky to lose to Bridgend in the 1982 Schweppes Welsh Cup semi-final.

Testimony of the persuasive side of Bevan's personality is found in the current Aberavon fly-half, Mike Lewis. Lewis blossomed from being erratic into just about the most exciting and penetrative fly-half in Welsh rugby, and his brilliant solo effort, which saw him slip through the Bridgend defence in the semi-final, was a try Phil

Gerald Williams passes as Roy Laidlaw closes in.

Graham Price leaps for
Wales against France.

Steve Sutton tries to power through for Wales.

Bennett would have been proud of. Lewis, along with Bridgend's Gary Pearce, and Swansea's Malcolm Dacey, are prepared to run at the opposition when the opportunity presents itself, and they are definitely John Bevan's type of players.

Throughout the season the Welsh forwards were never dominated, though equally, they were unable to dominate. But that's par for the course these days. The front row of Graham Price, Alan Phillips and Ian Stephens was rock solid and dependable in the scrums, but with so many permutations at lock, there was never any cohesive drive. With the reign of Geoff Wheel and Alan Martin at an end, it suddenly dawned that the cupboard was bare of strong young locks, for during the season Wheel, Moriarty, Steve Sutton and Robert Norster filled the positions, with Moriarty being the only one present during the whole campaign.

Moriarty reminds me a great deal of that marvellous Scottish servant, Alistair McHarg, in that he can combine the more earthy duties of lock forward with some inspired moments in the loose, and I, for one, would like to see him being given his chance at No. 8 this season.

Pontypool's beanpole lock Steve Sutton replaced the injured Wheel against France and had a dream debut. It's a long time since a Welsh lock gave an exhibition of two-handed catching, as did Sutton that day, but on closer examination it was plainly obvious that the French locks, Revlier in particular, had no interest whatsoever in contesting any of the lineouts. No one could deny Sutton's display — it was superb. Largely due to Sutton's dominance, Wales were able to overcome Serge Blanco's marvellous opening score and through sheer persistency wore the French down. With Holmes at the helm, they gained a deserved win to wipe out some of the memory of Dublin.

The Welsh back row, which had seen the recall of Clive Burgess for Swansea's Mark Davies on the blind side, and Rhodri Lewis for Gareth Williams, gave this vital unit more muscle and speed. Burgess, as ever, was constantly a

yard away from the action, and whenever there was a 50-50 ball to be won, Burgess seemed to claim this priceless possession with astonishing regularity.

Lewis, on the other hand, is the ideal modern open side flanker and his best will only be seen when Wales are able to play a more expansive, running game. Lewis is in the John Taylor mould, for he possesses tremendous pace and runs fine angles both in defence and in support play, as was seen at Twickenham when he was instantly available to take Alan Donovan's pass to score.

Lewis is not all muscle and pace, for he has already demonstrated his ability to read situations — knowing exactly when to run and link; indeed, some of the best

Rhodri Lewis beats Hare to score for Wales.

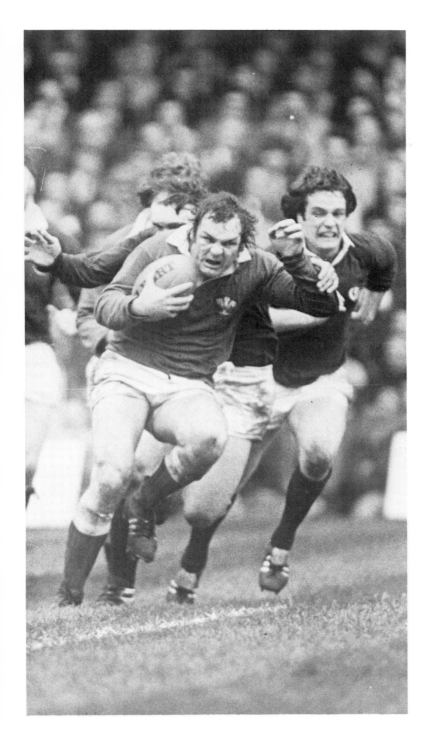

Clive Burgess on the
rampage.

passes delivered by a Welsh player last season were by him. Against France, it was his clean deflections to Jeff Squire which caught the eye, but if he has one slight weakness, it's his impatience in wanting to support play, when his first duty is to "nail" his man. A quiet word from the coach should easily do the trick. Without question, Lewis is here to stay.

Jeff Squire, in the key position of No. 8, had a very average season by his standards, and when injury prevented his playing against Scotland — Pontypool clubmate Eddie Butler deputising — one immediately wondered if the end of a marvellous international career had arrived. Squire has played almost continuous rugby for five or six years now and it showed, for his sharpness was severely blunted. He is still a colossal figure in the tight, but his legs are much heavier, and mobility and reaction have consequently suffered.

The most worrying feature of the Welsh forward play was their insistence on holding on to possession, which took away all element of surprise and allowed the opposition ample time to deploy and pick up defensive positions.

The Welsh back line failed to excite and trigger the imagination, even when the opportunity arose.

Cardiff's Pat Daniels, who had been tried previously in non-international games on the wing, was given his chance in his favourite centre position against Australia. Daniels can best be described as "explosive", and reacts well to someone else's promptings. He demonstrated this to perfection when taking a long flat pass from Gareth Davies 20 yards out, only to be denied a debut try by the superb Wallaby cover defence. Daniels retained his place against Ireland, but was then replaced by Llanelli's greatest character, Ray Gravell.

The "old duo" of Gravell and David Richards was restored to face the French, for it was felt that the Frenchmen's great dislike of Gravell's physical presence was again likely to upset their ranks. In fact, Gravell did play a major part in making the decisive opening Welsh try, when giving a delicate inside pass to Robert Ackerman, who transferred to Holmes. But what was again abundantly clear was the lack of fluency, understanding and speed of operation amongst the Welsh three-quarters.

David Richards, who, 12 months earlier, had displayed Nureyev's grace and balance in evading would-be French tackles when scoring a marvellous try, was laden-footed and totally lacking in confidence. Richards has been Wales' main source of inspiration in broken play, for he reacts brilliantly to the half gap; but, sadly, he seemed very reluctant to look for these situations to exploit. Richards suffered a hamstring injury before facing England and so Swansea clubmate Alan Donovan linked with Gravell.

Donovan, who has overcome many serious knee injuries, is a gifted footballer, and his inclusion against England balanced the midfield for he can "make" those

Gravell tackled by Rutherford in the Wales v. Scotland game 1982.

Gwyn Evans, Wales No.
15.

around him play — just as John Dawes used to. Unfortunately, opportunities were few and far between.

Wings Clive Rees and Robert Ackerman suffered the same fate, and had to settle for defensive duties throughout the season. Rees has genuine pace, but Ackerman still has to prove himself, looking a little lethargic when compared with the Scottish speedboys.

After Holmes, full back Gwyn Evans was Wales' best player. Evans, who has been converted from fly-half to full back, proved a worthy successor to J.P.R. Indeed, his entry into the line was Wales' only option outside the scrum, and on two occasions he crossed the line only to lose possession. Of course, his goalkicking was immaculate, and kept Wales in the hunt on several occasions, but for him to develop and provide an even better attacking edge, the Welsh handling in midfield must improve considerably.

The Schweppes Welsh Cup Final, which saw Cardiff retain the trophy, thanks to Ian Eidman's try in the 12-12 draw with Bridgend, threw up one of the most exciting runners seen in Welsh rugby for many a year: Bridgend's Mark Titley. Formerly with London Welsh, he showed terrific pace, and the way he took on his man and stepped out of a tackle reminded all watching of Gerald Davies.

Although there is a great deal of rethinking to be done I do believe that there is sufficient young talent available to rectify the situation — but it must be encouraged.

Llanelli has Kevin Thomas, Mark Douglas and Martin Gravell; Aberavon has Mike Lewis and Gary Matthews; Cardiff has the trio of Owen Golding, Bob Lakin and Kevin Edwards; whilst Swansea has Gareth John and Malcolm Dacey.

These young players, and those like Nathan Humphries and Aled Williams of the Welsh Secondary Schools, are my reason for optimism.

2
MAGIC MOMENTS

Chris Rea

The belief that Scotland's victory over Wales at Cardiff had been conceived on the paddocks of New Zealand the previous summer is not as far fetched as it sounds. Despite losing both Tests, the second by a try count of 7-1, the Scots had impressed many knowledgeable Kiwis with the quality of their play, particularly in the ruck, a phase of play which can count Jim Telfer as its most enthusiastic convert.

An acknowledged stifler of rucks in his playing days, Telfer, in his two years as Scottish coach, has come to realise that the Scots' best chance of success lies in winning quick, clean possession in the loose. Not since the days of McLauchlan, Carmichael and Brown have the Scots been able to dominate the tight, forward exchanges, and although the present pack improved as the season progressed, the strength of the side lay elsewhere.

There were no better loose forwards in the international championship than David Leslie and Jim Calder. Similar in style, they nevertheless complemented one another: Calder an effective custodian on the left-hand side of the scrum; and Leslie, an exceptionally gifted footballer, pounding his beat from the tail of the lineout. Furthermore, Leslie was the most reliable source of line-out possession.His season was once again shortened by injury, a broken leg forcing him to miss the matches against Ireland, France and Wales, but by that time the Scots had established their pattern of play, and the discovery of Derek White, who played against France and Wales, was a bonus.

Telfer was further helped in his tactical plans by the form of Roy Laidlaw at scrum-half. He was Scotland's most consistent performer behind the scrum, never afraid to engage the opposition back row and swift to see an opening. Rutherford's try against Ireland, an inspired moment in an otherwise dismal encounter, owed everything to Laidlaw's perception.

Rutherford, a talented, sensitive stand-off, had been burdened midway through the season by a spell of indifferent form, but came out of it in time for Cardiff. Possibly he had suffered from the Scots' approach to the game against the Wallabies.

Roy Laidlaw tackled.

Roy Laidlaw passes back to his line. (Scotland v. Romania)

In their match against the Australians, Ireland, with Tony Ward at stand-off, had given the most tactically inept display of the season. Whatever the weaknesses of the tourists, midfield defence was not one of them, and the determination of the Irish backs to try to prove otherwise was utterly perverse.

When Scotland's turn came, therefore, they were committed to pursuing a different course. The game would have to be played tight, with Rutherford controlling his urge to run with the ball. His kicks would have to be varied and always with a view to repossession, bearing in mind the Wallabies' facility for counter attack. In the event he kicked well, and the Scots won comfortably enough, although the try count of 3-1 against them moved Andy Irvine to comment afterwards that it was perhaps time to take a long hard look at the laws. As the season progressed many more were to voice similar opinions.

By playing a game which was unfamiliar to

him, Rutherford appeared unsure of himself in Scotland's next match, which was the Calcutta Cup. Twice, from favourable positions, he missed the opportunity to drop goals, and at no time did he show any inclination to test England's back row defence, which had to be vulnerable. Winterbottom was playing in his first international championship match, and neither Jeavons on the blind side nor Hesford at No. 8 could be described as seasoned veterans.

Tryless, the game was very much one of its time. There could be no doubting the commitment of the players, who deserved the highest praise for their defensive excellence. But where were the imagination and the sense of adventure upon which the game thrives? Lost perhaps in the labyrinth of squad sessions, video sessions and other modern aids.

The depressing thought occurred that the power to destroy had overcome the will to create. How would Gerald Davies have fared against such tackling? Would Barry John have been able to glide past the blanket defences of today? John had no doubt — defences were there to be beaten, awaiting only the individuals to unlock them. Rutherford, had the necessary skill, but he had looked confused against England and had lost his sense of time and timing. John was adamant that no matter how efficient the defence, the stand-off remained the most influential member of any rugby side, with the power to shape the game as he saw fit. The proof of John's words was provided by Ollie Campbell who, almost single handed, destroyed Wales and three weeks later did much the same to England.

Gradually, Rutherford began to take more upon himself, and his stage management of affairs behind the scrum

John Rutherford gets past Gareth Davies. (Cardiff v. Barbarians)

Rutherford scores
Scotland's first try
against France.

at Cardiff was indicative of a man in whom confidence abounds. Scotland's display that day was the culmination of Telfer's work over the previous two years. The victory itself, after a wait of twenty years, was of course an occasion to celebrate, but far more important was the manner of the victory. The rapier had proved superior to the cudgel. Wales, for once, had failed to move with the times. Their midfield had muscle but no guile, their homework had been slapdash.

David Johnston's defensive frailty against Gravell in the Centenary match two seasons ago was a distant memory to those who watched him cut down opponents of every size last season. True, Johnston, like Rutherford, had shown signs of uncertainty during the campaign – his failure to take the gap offered to him by England being the most glaring error of judgement. But he too was well on the way to complete rehabilitation before Cardiff.

In the early part of the season the Australians had adapted far more readily to the new tackle law than

British players, and had demonstrated time and again the advantages not only of good midfield defence, but also of countering support. By the time they met Wales, Scotland had learned the lesson well. Johnston and Renwick were impregnable in defence and in attack the Scots were a couple of yards faster.

Against Wales Jim Renwick gave what was the finest exhibition I have seen from an international centre, and in so doing rounded off what has been his most successful season. He led his club Hawick to their sixth title in the Schweppes National Leagues, and finished up top points scorer with 134 from 11 matches. If Hawick owed him a colossal debt, so did Scotland. His drop goal against France turned the match Scotland's way; his drop goal against Wales, struck to perfection, was equally crucial.

For Andy Irvine it was a relatively uneventful series, but his role was nonetheless important. His very presence was enough to concentrate the minds of the opposition. By lurking menacingly in the shadows he was the ideal

Jim Pollock, one of Scotland's new centres.

Jim Renwick looks for
the opening.

decoy, allowing more time and space for Rutherford, Johnston, Renwick and the newcomer, Roger Baird.

It was Baird's ingenuity which put the Scots on the right lines against Wales, and yet who could have blamed this 21 year-old if, on his first appearance at Cardiff and with the match not ten minutes old, he had put the ball safely into touch? His audacity typified the Scots' attitude that day. Against the Irish the Scots had been drained both mentally and physically by the ballyhoo surrounding Ireland's Triple Crown bid. When the time came to take the field they, not the Irish, were the closer to nervous exhaustion. Staying in the same hotel as their opponents cannot have helped, and the time has surely come for this Dublin tradition to be terminated.

Johnston scores for Scotland.

Baird kicks to safety.

Johnston scores for
Scotland against Wales.

The build up to the Welsh match was an altogether
more placid affair. Telfer himself was more relaxed, and
the players were encouraged to do what came naturally to
them. The result was immensely gratifying to Scotland
and, it is to be hoped, an example for other countries to
follow.

Sadly, the preoccupation with forward power is still
with us, despite the fact that we have seen two Lions sides
win the forward exchanges but lose the series. It is now
ten years since Colin Mead wrote, "I see Britain as being
in a unique position in world rugby, but I wonder if the
British themselves appreciate it. New strength in the
forwards has not automatically cancelled out brilliance in

Andy Irvine kicks one of
his penalties for
Scotland on his way to a
point scoring record.
(Scotland v. Australia)

the backs. So why not use the new to exploit the traditional? That seems to make a lot of rugby sense to me." Had Mead been at the National Stadium in March to witness the wretched attempts of the Welsh backs to move the ball to the wings he would indeed have considered that the rugby world had gone mad.

Apart from Scotland's final flourish there was very little else to enthuse over during the season. Scotland B suffered annihilation against France B and confirmed fears that there is precious little cover in the event of injury, plague or pestilence befalling those who are at present in the senior side. Lower down the scale the Scottish Schools were badly beaten in all their matches, the heaviest defeats being inflicted by Wales, Ireland and Australia who, it must be added, were able to field a pack of forwards much heavier than those who had represented the full Wallaby side earlier in the season. The Scottish Under 21s fared little better, their defeat by an equally unimaginative Scottish Universities XV being a strong inducement to young men to golf, ski, shop with mum or do anything other than play rugby.

The top three clubs were Hawick, Heriots and Gala, the only three to have won the First Division title, which proves that little has changed since the inception of the leagues nine years ago. The change that will be made this coming season is very definitely for the worse. The preposterous decision has been taken to increase the numbers in each of the seven leagues from 12 to 14. This will enable the clubs to play 13 matches instead of 11 which, it is argued, will give those clubs threatened by relegation a stay of execution at least until the latter part of the season. Hardly positive thinking.

What appears to have been overlooked is that the addition of a number of inferior clubs will eventually lead to a decline in standards. Much better to have reduced the numbers in each league to eight and to have played on a home and away basis.

Further afield, the enforced retirement of Bill Beaumont was a cruel blow. The game is not so well endowed with gentlemen that it can afford to lose one of Beaumont's calibre.

The pre-eminence of the penalty kick was, however, the most depressing aspect of the season, the nadir coming at Lansdowne Road when Ireland through Ollie Campbell kicked their way to victory over Scotland and to their first Triple Crown since 1949. The Scots, who were penalised in the ratio of 2-1, had no complaints afterwards about Clive Norling's refereeing. They had only themselves to blame, and throughout the season they conceded too many penalties. It is worth noting that in the Irish match two thirds of the penalties were given for offside or for players coming over the top in the rucks, which does suggest that the tackle law, although an improvement on the previous law, still requires adjustment. It is a devilishly hard law to apply with any degree of consistency and for that reason alone deserves another look from the legislators.

Deans and Milne close on the ball.

Robertson and Milne at work in the line.

The variable quality of the refereeing throughout the season perhaps reflected the mediocrity of the play, but there is an alarming tendency for the referee to consider himself the principal character on the stage. The posturings and antics of some are quite unacceptable and have more in common with those who officiate at soccer matches. There were a couple of occasions during the international season when a touch judge encroached on to the field of play in order to bring the referee's attention to an infringement. The old adage, that the best referees are those who are seen and heard least, still applies.

The incident which aroused most feeling occurred in the Scotland-Australia match at Murrayfield, when Tony Shaw, the Wallabies' captain, took a swipe at Bill Cuthbertson in full view of the spectators and underneath the nose of the referee Roger Quittendon. Quittendon was severely criticised for not sending Shaw from the field, and yet, for me, an act which was clearly born of momentary frustration was far less distasteful than that by a Scottish forward who, later in the season, sank his boot into the back of an opponent on the blind side of the referee. The touch judge on that occasion chose to remain silent.

Rugby is treading a difficult path at present. It cannot survive without financial aid, but at a time when sport and sportsmen are highly profitable commodities, the problem of how to be commercially aware without destroying the ethos of the game is one that appears to be beyond the administrators. The anomalies are endless. Players who have retired from the game but who have accepted money for writing or broadcasting are cast out, usually amidst a fanfare of self-righteousness from the union concerned, and yet the unions, like everyone else connected with the game, know only too well that current players are receiving money for endorsing certain products.

There are mutterings, louder and more plausible with each new season, that the top players have a right to some financial gain from a game which now demands so much of their time. Rugby, we are constantly being told, is a game for the players, but that does not mean that the players should gain materially from it. Rugby, as I understand it, is for fun and for the friendships formed. For the international player it is surely reward enough to have played and to have won or tried to win, for his country.

3
A HUNDRED YEARS OF THE VARSITY GAME

Gerald Davies

When the clock stands at 10 to 3 on the second Tuesday in December, no Oxford or Cambridge man has time to wonder, as Rupert Brooke once did, whether there is honey still for tea. The Varsity match, having started at 2.15, has five nervous minutes to go to half-time, and to think of such casual and idle pleasures would show a remarkable indifference even by those who did not attend either University. That would be in the normal course of things, and for 99 Varsity matches normality did reign, at least as far as the weather was concerned. Invariably, the day is dark, the sky wearing its clouds like a shroud, hanging so heavy and low that the aircraft bound on its flight path to Heathrow is heard but rarely seen. It might on occasions rain or the wind might blow. Or the sly sun, however fleetingly, may appear, like royalty, to give its blessing. But for the hundredth Varsity match, it was, perversely, the snow, not the sun, that turned up with Prince Andrew. The snow, lots of it, came for the first time and transformed the green turf to a virginal whiteness. As if appearing in some detergent advert, the light blue and white of Cambridge looked suddenly more appealing and attractive than Oxford's dark blue strip, contrasting with the snowy vastness of the surrounding scene as if cast by a Hollywood mogul in whose 'B' movie the villains were always dressed in sombre colours.

But the villain of the piece on this occasion was the snow, which contrived to make a travesty of the match. The 30 players contested bravely to make something of it but the several inches of snow proved an impossible obstacle. There was little to retain the interest of even the most partisan supporter. And so, in contrast to other years, there were many who had their minds on other matters, like the evening's celebrity dinner at the Hilton, who for the first time were left to wish for some honey and a hot pot of tea to warm the body and to revive a despondent spirit. There was faint hope that we would ever see anything remotely resembling a rugby match.

Spot the ball!

Brooks tries to break through.

Once having grown accustomed to the peculiar and eccentric nature of the setting and having exhausted my store of pleasantries with my neighbour in the stand, there was nothing much else to do except cast my mind back, fitfully, to my own days at Cambridge.

Memories of those times are becoming vague although all those Fellows and tutors I once knew may have claimed even then in the privacy of their own senior common room that the particular faculty which summons up details and images of the distant, or even immediate past could never be considered a strong point of mine. Memories, as I say, are somewhat dim and shadowy, like the less-than-glorious monochrome reproductions of an old but favourite, easy-to-work-with camera. Faces of the

Derek Wyatt hands off Huw Davies.

time are ill-defined, and can never be reconstructed from or equated with the glossy physiognomies of the jolly, portly fellows they have suddenly become. Actions, too, once so clear, become mistily obscure so that they are quite easily forgotten, or conversely, because of their sheer vagueness, are elevated with legend. The mood, like someone's surreptitious wink across a crowded room, can be definite but so fleeting. Even the names, familiar as I was with the many Jones and Evans in my own village whose trade was their sole distinguishing feature, had a curious cadence which seemed to echo a likely future employment. Saville and Page might represent some firm of fashionable designers from Knightsbridge, Jordan and Hughes a high-sounding High Street store; Rodgers and Redmond might revive a late forties music-hall entertainment, whilst encapsulated in the name Keith-Roach was a whole retinue of marketing consultants. And Shackleton and Spencer could represent nothing less than the best brewed beer in Yorkshire.

However fanciful all this might prove to be, the records and statistics remain a secure testimony that it all did take place — once upon a time. They are also a reminder of things I would rather forget, for example my term of captaincy. When the facts of that year are recalled I prefer to dwell instead on the beautiful ochre-coloured autumn we had, and to think of the many victories we tucked under our belts during the term. Peter Carroll, the Oxford captain, has always forgiven me for glossing over the details of the match itself. It was he, with a 14-3 win who took home the garland that day.

I was on the winning side only once, in 1968. In that year and on that day I remember well the pre-match build up. There were bystanders at every one of the dozen or so traffic lights from Windsor, where we had stayed overnight, to the Pope's Grotto in Richmond, where we were due for lunch, who doubtless heard the raucous rallying cry of the Cambridge crowd in the bus preparing for the fray against Oxford. We must have seemed a common lot

Looking for the ball.

to them and an uncommon sight to behold, bedecked as we all were, on that dark December day, in flamboyant and unfashionable light blue blazers, on our way to lunch in a dining room full of light blue carnations.

To those bystanders, the rallying call was a simple and innocent abbreviation, an arbitrary selection of letters from the alphabet, it seemed. G.D.B.O. — to the bright blue boys inside, reared on something better and wittier, they unsubtly and uncompromisingly stood for *God Damn Bloody Oxford.* Another set of traffic lights and Derek Lyons, our captain, demanded, for that was the custom, lound and fearless, a G.D.B.O., as if attempting to call up from the depths the spirit of some unfamiliar hate. Oxford were our enemy, not only to be subdued, but also to be crushed and conquered. Never a one to be too demonstrative in these matters, and preferring to dwell instead on the evening's likely entertainment in Quaglino's, I whispered the letters into my scarf, all the way from our watering hole in Windsor to the peace and calm of the Pope's Grotto, glad of the respite, the ordeal over. Let's just get on with the game, lads. But, by then it was clear that it might be too frivolous to consider it merely as a game.

The attitude was confirmed later on in the dressing room. The appeal to our feelings of hate engendered in the bus was cunningly replaced by a full, heated and fervent appeal to our feelings of undying love for our alma mater. Unlike our antics in the bus, that approach had a familiar ring to it. A non-conformist, rugby-playing Welshman enjoys a full-blooded and uncompromising sermon; something to get your teeth into and to get the heart and emotions ticking over at a fair lick. To those

C. Biddell (Cambridge) wins a lineout.

brought up in the elegant, traditional style of the Church of England, it might not have been so, but after the team talk in 1968 I acknowledged that sometimes they will quite happily and conveniently forget the charm and elegance. Such an appreciation of order and ritual are unsuited to a rugby changing room, and perhaps the sheer histrionics of a fire and brimstone sermon, more renowned in the valleys of Wales than the downs of rural England, are closer to what is required fifteen minutes before kick-off!

But there was no need for divine inspiration or, as it turned out, divine intervention. Our captain took a secular theme from a secular text — Shakespeare's *Henry V* and the motivating cry at Agincourt. It was close enough to the real thing. The appeal, paraphrased, was to the few, the happy few, the band of brothers, and of the story the good man shall teach his son in years to come. It was so close to the rich style and theme of Clive Rowlands that I felt quite at home. Not that Clive, mind you, was ever likely to quote the Scriptures or even Shakespeare for that matter. He preferred, above all else, a more original script, thought up in his own fair mind. Although the skeleton of the text may have been fashioned beforehand, he preferred to add the flesh as he was going along, inspired by his own eloquence. He liked to use the occasional quotation, for effect and for driving the point home. Essentially, his was a homespun philosophy, straight ·and to the point. He would quote a village pundit, perhaps, or better still, a London journalist or two who might not hold the same faith as he did in the Welsh team. Barry John in the meantime was thinking of the next race at Doncaster. Rugby team talks are all things to all men. At any rate, I had not heard Shakespeare quoted before — or since. But then I had not been to Cambridge before, nor had I been in a team captained by an Englishman. Was this kind of thing normal, I wondered? By the time Derek Lyons finished, all that remained for all of us in that dressing room was to stand up and sing "Land of Hope and Glory". We didn't. But we did go on to win.

So that win in my first year was balanced with a loss in my final year. Looking back more benevolently, the occasion was more important than the final outcome. It is not that winning is made too important but that losing should be considered so tragic!

What of the Varsity match now that it embarks on its second century of games? There are a good many people who are indifferent, even hostile, towards it. They find it quite unacceptable that such a match should receive the publicity and pre-eminence that it does believing that it has outgrown its value. The universities, once the equal of first-class clubs, are no longer capable of sustaining a high-level performance, or so the argument runs. I have no wish to enter too fully into that particular debate except to say this the promotion of other people's claims should not be done at the expense of Oxford and Cambridge, nor should the Varsity match itself be devalued. In a society which aims for equality, I believe the tendency is to level down the standards of those at the top instead of making the effort to raise the standards of others. Excellence in all walks of life should be encouraged and should not be considered, as it so often is, as an unfair and dubious privilege. Someone somewhere should and must set the standard. The universities are places where academics as well as sporting excellence can be nurtured. They are places to pursue ideals. Bannister, Brasher and Chataway did so when they set out to break the four minute mile. So did the Corinthian Casuals pursue the ideal of sportsmanship in soccer, which is so rapidly in decline nowadays. The Boat Race, a curious anachronism to many, still epitomises courage and fitness, endeavour and skill, in much the same way that the rugby match does.

If such standards could be set yesterday, then why not today or tomorrow? Both Oxford and Cambridge, with their system of independent colleges, have it well within their compass to produce sporting as well as academic achievement. Indeed, so have all the universities and colleges throughout the land. The admissions tutors would do well to consider such a policy. The essence of sportsmanship, whatever some may think, is an ideal well worth pursuing, as is the pursuit of academic excellence.

Mens Sana, in Corpore Sano est.
(A Sound Mind in a Sound Body)

4
A YEAR OF TRIUMPH

Ray McLaughlin

Most ex-international rugby players suffer from the weakness of continuing to nurture the thought that the teams of today may not be as good as the teams of yesteryear. The theme that "things ain't what they used to be" is always close to the surface when those men of the past meet on international night to evaluate the events of the day.

Foremost amongst the Irish ex-internationals who have had good reason to entertain that theme are the men of 1949. The heroes of the Double Triple Crown winning team are for the most part alive and well. The unique glory of being members of Ireland's last Triple Crown winning side had stayed with them over the years and the distinction had long since adopted an eternal and ever-lasting look. Even they, despite a natural bias, must have progressed through the past 37 years in a state of increasing bewilderment as successive Irish teams failed to achieve what must have seemed to them to be a fairly simple task — to win three matches in a row. Surely these men have had a very legitimate basis for taking the view that Irish teams of the recent past were not as good as Irish teams of earlier days.

Of course, this theme has had particularly fertile ground in which to flourish over recent years. Apart from Colin Patterson's great year, the period from 1976 to

1982 had been a period of continuing failure on the playing field. There was good reason for the ex-player to nod his head on Saturday night and indulge in the sentiment "God be with the days".

Then we came to January 1982 as Ireland set about another international campaign. The average Irish rugby follower is very much an optimist, but on this occasion there were few who believed that this would be the season to end the Triple Crown famine, and I have no doubt that Karl Mullen, Jim McCarthy and their colleagues felt that their unique status would survive intact for yet another year. Ireland had gone eight matches without a win. Their last match had produced a very disappointing performance against Australia. There was a feeling of disillusionment across the board, and there was limited evidence of optimism in the previews of the season published by our established scribes.

Yet those who were a bit closer to events could see some positive signs. Ciaran Fitzgerald was back in the

Lenihan feeds McGrath against England.

MacNeill's try
against England.

team. The new find in the second row, Donal Lenihan,
looked a man with exceptional talent. Fergus Slattery was
not now carrying the burden of captaincy and could be
expected to produce new found enthusiasm. The
selectors had finally abandoned the attempt to include
both Tony Ward and Ollie Campbell in the same team,
and the new wing appointments, Ringland and Finn, held
out a lot of promise.

As the season developed the feeling that better things
were to come seemed to have an increasingly valid basis.
We won our first match against Wales, and even at that
stage we began to hear murmurs about the Triple Crown.
Irish rugby followers are forever expectant and they only
need to see the faintest light at the end of the tunnel to
start talking about the elusive prize. For them every year
is a year of hope.

However, to those in the business of looking at the
detail, the win against Wales, though impressive, nevertheless offered only a limited basis for confidence. Ireland

had defeated Wales even more comprehensively two years before and most people acknowledged that the 1982 Welsh team was a particularly weak one. Furthermore, the game could have swung the opposite way if Wales hadn't thrown away a certain try shortly before half time, and of course the departure of Gareth Davies was also a significant factor in Ireland's favour. Yes, certainly Ireland's performance was competent and efficient and it produced some sparkling moments, but everybody knew that the big test was yet to come.

It came at Twickenham on February 6th. If there was a weakness in this Irish team it was generally thought to be in the tight forward play, and if there was a team that was going to exploit that weakness it would be England.

However, as the match drew nearer the omens seemed to be good. Nobody would wish Bill Beaumont any ill will but it was certainly no hardship for any Irish man to entertain the thought of an English team minus Bill Beaumont. There was a question mark over the fitness of John Scott and then at the last moment Paul Dodge also disappeared from the scene. The loss of some of England's biggest guns, together with a possible erosion of confidence due to change of leadership, and the fact that the statistics were in Ireland's favour, all added up to a feeling of optimism in the Irish camp.

On the day, the optimism proved to be justified. Even though England laboured from the handicap of the late changes in personnel, there can be no denying that this was an impressive performance by an increasingly impressive Irish team. Even though Bill Beaumont was missing, it was still a formidable English pack, and perhaps the principal factor determining Ireland's victory was the way in which the Irish pack met the English challenge and contested every inch of ground in every phase of play.

England scored a late try, so that Ireland eventually won by only the narrowest of margins, but few people disputed the view that the margin belied the difference on

Ciaran Fitzgerald,
captain of inspiration.

the day and that Ireland were well worthy of their win.

So we were all set for the crucial match against Scotland. Surely if we were ever to win another Triple Crown, this had to be the time. Only twice in the previous 33 years had Ireland the opportunity of winning a Triple Crown as they went into the last match, and those occasions were in 1965 and 1969. On both occasions we were up against a formidable Welsh opposition and on both occasions the match was played at Cardiff. Now the venue was Lansdowne Road and the opposition was Scotland, who were thought by many to be the weakest of the five countries. Scotland had not won an away match in their previous 20 away games and there seemed to be no good reason why they should reverse that trend on this occasion. With Campbell in top form and with the absolute certainty that he would indulge in no unnecessary frills, and with Irish confidence riding very high, I for one thought that the odds should be three to one against Scotland, and of course they are dangerous odds to quote in the context of any international rugby match.

I know that Ciaran Fitzgerald and his men were uneasy about the excessive confidence that prevailed, but as far as the general public was concerned the matter was a foregone conclusion. Triple Crown ties were available for sale in the week before the match and people talked as if the game had been played and won. The match coincided with the general election in Ireland and interest in the election was totally eclipsed by the sense of anticipation created by the prospect of a Triple Crown.

Des O'Brien spoke to the nation from his home in Edinburgh. Karl Mullen, who was captain of the 1949 side, exchanged views with Ciaran Fitzgerald on television. Men appeared out of the woodwork who were thought to have long since passed away, and the media resurrected others who hadn't been seen for twenty years. They gave their views on radio and television on just about every night of the week, and the papers were dominated by stories about the Triple Crown campaigns of 1948 and 1949.

Altogether it was a great week. People put their problems aside and joined in the national dialogue. There was very little work done, and with Ireland's economy in the worst state that it had been in for twenty years, the occasion brought much-needed cheer.

Finally, we came to Saturday February 20th. In the event, Scotland were demolished. I found myself thinking afterwards that it was the worst display by an international pack that I had ever seen. Yet it must be remembered that virtually the same Scottish pack had outplayed the Welsh pack in Cardiff, had given England a good fight at Murrayfield, and were well on top of the French pack, also at Murrayfield. Perhaps they were below form on the day but I think it is nearer the truth to say that they were given little chance to compete by an Irish team that was brought to the match tuned to the nth degree and by an Irish pack that played to the maximum of efficiency and endeavour.

The game was a disappointment in that it didn't have the flourish and the sparkle of the earlier games. Many were critical of the fact that all of Ireland's 21 points were scored without crossing the Scottish line, and there was particular disappointment that the only try of the match had been scored by the vanquished. Perhaps disappointment in the game was justified but I think the criticism was not. Clearly I am biased, but if the opposition insists on giving away penalties every time you get into an attacking position you cannot be expected to score tries. If the opposition kicks off from the half-way line you are inevitably in a defensive position, and it takes time to develop from there to an attacking position. Lineout balls must be secured, scrums must be won, possession must be run or kicked.

When a team gets into an attacking position, it cannot hope that the first piece of possession it gets will be a piece that it is possible to do something constructive with. And even if the opposition is determined to concede a penalty it will take them some time to do that. Then when the penalty is conceded it takes time to set the ball up and take the kick, and it takes the opposition time to collect it, return to the half-way line and set play in motion once again.

I estimated the amount of time that all of this sequence would take and I suggest that in average circumstances it could be as long as six minutes. On the day, Ireland missed three penalties, so altogether there were nine occasions when Ireland were in an attacking position and were denied the opportunity of an assault on the Scottish line. That was over 50 minutes of play during which attack was not possible, and when you consider that the other team has to have its share of attacking time also, I think it is unrealistic to criticise Ireland for not putting on an attacking show. As I saw the match, Ireland did the job asked of them in a comprehensive way and I don't think they could have been asked to do any more.

Inevitably at the end of it all people began to ask the question, "What is so great about winning three matches in a row? Liverpool, Manchester United and several other First Division soccer clubs do it all of the time". Of course it is a stupid question because all we have to do is look at the last 33 years to realise that it is an extremely difficult task and that 32 previous Irish teams had tried and failed. It was indeed an historic success based on a combination of excellent team performance and excellent individual performances.

It is interesting to reflect on the ingredients of this success. Of course the on-field individual performances constitute the principal factor, but nowadays success must be based on an appropriate combination of good play, good coaching, good selection and good captaincy.

Ciaran Fitzgerald was made captain and he took his opportunity well. He stamped his own authority on the situation straightaway without fuss and without noise. He imposed his own approach on the handling of the team and he won our admiration for the fine way he led the team both on and off the field.

The coach always plays a major role in creating the environment and conditions necessary to enable the team to perform, and Tom Kiernan's management of the team and his influence on the preparation and pattern of play played a vital part in the ultimate success. During Tom's initial period as coach he was beset by a run of bad luck but nevertheless it was an inauspicious start and sufficient to deal a body blow to the confidence of lesser men. It is a tribute to Tom's character that he could recover from that to demand and win from his players the necessary respect and to create the conditions in which their performance would prosper.

Ireland/Scotland lineout problems.

I would like to pay a particular tribute to the selectors. The Irish team which won the Triple Crown was different in nine positions from the team of the previous year. Since when have we seen any international selection committee make nine changes and get the formula absolutely right all at once? Our selectors are abused only too quickly when things go wrong and seldom get any credit when things go right. Ireland has been blessed over the years with a series of very good selection committees and I would like to compliment Kevin Flynn, P. J. Dwyer and co on a job well done.

The players themselves are the people who play the game and produce the results. All our players fulfilled their roles to a highly satisfactory degree. It is hard to pick out heroes in a season such as this one but few would dispute that Ollie Campbell was the primary motive force. I have often said that Mike Gibson was the greatest player I have seen, but I think that the Triple Crown series saw the three best matches in succession by any Irish fly-half that I can recall.

Once you get away from Ollie Campbell you are down to the level of ordinary mortals. But some of these mortals were superb. Our back row had three excellent matches. I was particularly impressed with John O'Driscoll, who was a tower of strength during the season. Donal Lenihan had superb performances against England and Wales. Philip Orr has had a succession of great seasons in the loose but on some occasions he has had some problems in the tight. This year, however, he matched another great season in the loose with an excellent performance in the tight and in my view it was his best year.

Moss Finn played in a way which caused us to question why he hadn't been there for years, and Michael Kiernan confirmed that here indeed was a new talent with a long and promising future ahead of him.

Ciaran Fitzgerald's play matched the standard of his captaincy and Gerry McLoughlin was fitter than I have seen him. He was determined to recover from the disappointment of a bad performance against England two years before. In what better way could he have crowned that recovery than by scoring that marvellous try? Barry John suggested that the whole of Ireland helped him over but Gerry himself has a different view. He claims that he pulled the whole Irish team over with him so that they could share in the glory!

So we look ahead to next year and to the question which is clearly in the forefront of our minds — how good is this Irish team? I think the biggest question mark over the team is over the capacity of the tight five successfully to meet all the opposition that can be thrown at them. For years the Irish pack has had great flourish and venom in the loose and has tended to run into problems only when confronted by a pack such as England have had, which could potentially grind them in the tight, deny them the loose ball on which they flourish, and eventually sap their energy and enthusiasm. England failed to do that this year but France, spearheaded by Imbernon and Paparemborde, seemed to achieve it.

However, it is difficult to be too sure about that French match because it was only to be expected that Ireland would suffer some reaction following the Triple Crown success. Whether France would achieve the same success against the Irish pack on another day, when more would be at stake, is a question which must remain unanswered.

I think it would be wrong to call this a great Irish team. Great is a word to be reserved for teams with a certain minimum level of achievement. This is virtually a new team, relative to the previous year, and has had only one season in which to test itself. It has won three matches out of four but it has a lot to do before it can be considered a great team, in the way that the English team of the early sixties or the Welsh team of the early seventies were entitled to be called great. The question is whether it has the potential to become a great team by going on to win another Triple Crown or two over the next few years. The answer is not clear cut. Unfortunately, our reserve talent in some positions is thin on the ground. In my view we have, in Orr, McLoughlin and Fitzpatrick, three prop forwards who can compete at international level, but the standard beyond that is well below international level. If Orr does not go on for another year either because of retirement or injury, who will take over at loose head? And how vulnerable are we then, if either McLoughlin or Fitzpatrick are removed through injury, retirement, or any other reason?

Ciaran Fitzgerald has several years left in him but we must ask if Moss Keane has seen the end of the road. And if he has, what would our second row look like? Ireland has some competent second rows, of whom Gerry Holland is perhaps the best known, but if Moss Keane goes I cannot see any combination of two that will have a sufficiently imposing physical presence to stand up to all conditions. I know I may be guilty of comparing today

Moss Keane bursts past Alan Tomes.

with yesterday but Donal Lenihan and Gerry Holland are still a long way short of carrying the power that was carried by Willie John McBride. Donal Lenihan is certainly one of our biggest finds of the season. His lineout talent is perhaps the best that we have seen from an Irish second row forward for many years, but I question whether he is yet physically strong enough to stand up to all of the demands that can be made of him at international level. However, he is a determined young man, he has done a lot of weight training, and perhaps we will see a stronger and more physical Donal Lenihan over the next year or two.

Our back row has for many years been the strongest part of the pack. All three players have punched in one marvellous display after another. I know that Willie Duggan has the motivation to go for another year, and

John O'Driscoll fights for Ireland.

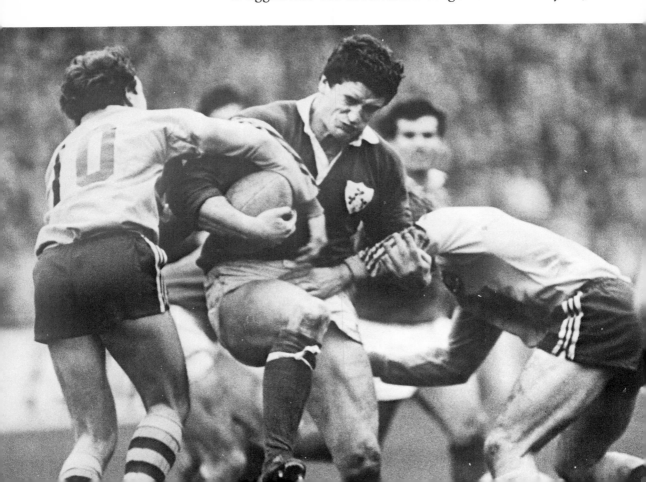

John O'Driscoll must surely be an automatic choice for several years ahead. The question mark hangs over Fergus Slattery. In my mind there is nobody around to match him if he gives the time and energy that is required, so I feel it is simply a question of motivation and availability of time. If he does decide to go again and put the effort into it, I have little doubt that we will, once more, have a series of superb back row performances from this Irish team.

I have always been an admirer of Robbie McGrath and I would have selected him before John Robbie last year. However I cannot help reflecting for a moment on what the position might have been if Colm Patterson had not received his unfortunate injury. I felt that Patterson was by far the best scrum-half that Ireland had on an international field since I can recall, and if his talents were added to a Campbell in top form we would surely have the best half back combination in Irish rugby history, and one capable of posing a threat to any opposition in any circumstances.

This year saw Moss Finn reach his true potential, and if David Irwin comes back on song to join the promising Kiernan in the centre we would then have a very young back line with a lot of promise, and certainly a combination to justify looking ahead with considerable confidence to the future.

In summary, I think we have a very competent back line which is clearly capable of rising to exceptional performance. We will have a very good back row, at least for another year, but I feel there may be some question marks over the tight five. Until those question marks have been removed we will have to reserve judgement about how far this Irish team can go. However, it remains true that we now have a lot of new talent and a lot of young blood in the team, and anybody with rugby close to his heart cannot but feel a stir of excitement as he looks forward to the next few years.

5
OLLIE CAMPBELL

Barry John

Mike Gibson, the most complete midfield player in modern times, once said, "The fly-half's attitude is also the team's".

Ollie Campbell must be a firm believer in Gibson's Law. Campbell totally transformed Ireland from Wooden Spoonists to being Triple Crown and championship winners and this as much by his attitude as by his vast range of beautiful skills. To my mind he was easily Europe's player of the year for the 1982 Home International series.

Campbell has always been a highly talented and gifted performer — a natural — who commanded great respect from his fellow players, so what made a volcano within him rage and then erupt?

Of course, his continued battle with Tony Ward must have had an inhibiting effect on his game, but I suspect that the fact that the Irish selectors opted for him rather than the equally gifted Ward, made Campbell throw caution to the wind and really give it a go. Moreover, Campbell had only played a couple of games to prove his fitness after a lengthy injury.

Campbell's display against Wales was a joy — a virtuoso performance of which any fly-half would have been proud. To me it is always a pleasure to see a sportsman do full justice to his talents and seek perfection when it really matters: Comaneci on the bars; Viv Richards in that dismissive mood even when against the best of attacks; or Diego Maradona making nonsense of his markers with a swing of the hips!

But to me, to see a fly-half read every situation correctly and take the correct option is a sight to behold. Campbell's play was full of guile, insinuation and threat. His every move was purposeful and the rest all around, those men in green, reacted instantly to his promptings.

Campbell seemed to fulfil the fly-half's brief to perfection. His performance that day made the Welsh defeat a little easier to take, for they had fallen to a master craftsman who was finding himself. I believe that the resurgence of the ageing Irish pack was due largely to the influence of Campbell. Undoubtedly new captain Ciaran Fitzgerald played his part, but I believe Willie Duggan,

Ireland's hero Ollie Campbell attempts a break past Calder and Johnston (12).

Ollie Campbell — master
kicker.

Moss Keane, John O'Driscoll, Phil Orr and Fergus Slattery responded to the presence of a man who was inspired.

Robbie McGrath is a dogged, resourceful scrum-half, but not the world's greatest passer. Campbell knew this and accommodated accordingly — his mind was geared to the fact that the ball could come at any angle! This was perfectly illustrated in the making of Ireland's first try against Wales, Campbell turned the imperfect pass into a glorious score. McGrath's pass was picked up ankle high, which stopped Campbell going open as was intended, but instead of the customary kick followed by various gesticulations, Campbell swept to the short side

R. McGrath — Campbell's provider.

and with perfect balance, raced through the Welsh cover to give Moss Finn the easiest of tries.

Campbell was heavily involved in the other two scores by Trevor Ringland and Finn again. He conceived Ringland's try with one of those perfectly weighted grubber kicks and his aggressive burst into the heart of the Welsh defence before linking with his backs gave Finn the overlap try.

Campbell had now arrived — when the fly-half is at the top of his game, the whole team reacts — Gibson's Law. His new-found confidence was evident at Twickenham. Perfectly placed kicks; timely probing runs; it was like conducting an orchestra, with confidence oozing out. His composure under pressure was proved beyond doubt when his dropped goal attempt was charged down, but his recovery, in which he produced two lightning-quick first-time touches sent McLaughlin, with the assistance of seemingly the whole of Ireland, charging over in the corner.

Campbell's general game was coming together like a jigsaw, and his prime weapon, the right boot, was working better than ever severely punishing the unsuspecting and the foolish. Even if all 21 points came via that dependable source to beat Scotland in the deciding Triple Crown encounter, Campbell and Ireland had shown in the emotionally charged atmosphere that day, and certainly in the previous two games, that they were a highly constructive and enterprising team, fully deserving of a place in the history books.

Campbell will, of course, be at the helm again for Ireland and will be a key figure for the 1983 Lions who will tour New Zealand.

6
BILLY BEAUMONT

John Taylor

The greatest compliment and accolade Billy Beaumont
could ever have wished for came from the English rugby
public when he was suddenly and unexpectedly forced to
announce his retirement. They were stunned. Nobody
questioned his decision; it was undoubtedly right and no
person in his right mind (despite the urgings of one over
zealous rugby writer) would have done otherwise. Nevertheless they still felt cheated.

What makes it all so surprising is that we are talking
about the English. When Barry John retired while still in
his prime Welsh supporters were mortified, and when
Mervyn Davies' wonderful talent was taken from them in
such dramatic fashion the whole nation was shattered.
But, William Blackledge Beaumont is from England and
they are generally more conservative in their praises and
emotions about rugby men.

When players have been deified they have always been
three-quarters, an Obolensky, a Butterfield, a Sharp or a
Duckham, and they have never come from north of
Birmingham. For a second row forward from
unfashionable Fylde, a club that does not even play
against many of the traditionally accepted "top clubs", to
have made such an impression speaks volumes for the job
which Billy Beaumont did for England.

When he took over the captaincy in 1978 they had not
won a championship since 1963, except for the peculiar
season of 1973 when all five nations won their home

Billy Beaumont in
action for the Lions
against the Springboks
(1980).

fixtures to make it a quintuple tie. They had to go back even further, to 1960, for their last Triple Crown, and to 1957 for the last Grand Slam. No wonder he became a national hero when they achived that feat again in 1980.

Some people have suggested that Beaumont was lucky, and that it was largely coincidence that his period of captaincy was accompanied by long overdue success for England. They point out that the English selectors had been criminally unfair on the players, that individuals were picked and discarded before they had had a chance to find their feet at the higher level, and that only when Budge Rogers took over as chairman did they adopt a policy of selecting a squad at the beginning of the campaign and then sticking with it.

Bill Beaumont, the England captain shouts with joy as the final whistle goes and Scott (8) lifts him in triumph and Rafter (7) joins in.

Beaumont and Rives —
still friends after all is
over.

Beaumont was certainly fortunate that Rogers also had the same thoughts about captaincy. Apart from one match at the beginning of 1979 when Roger Uttley was recalled as flanker and captain (he had missed the whole of the 1978 season because of injury), Rogers was loyal to Beaumont even though England certainly did not achieve instant success and there were plenty of other experienced players in the squad.

Fran Cotton freely admits to being amazed when the job was given to Billy. "Roger Uttley and Tony Neary were absent from the side but there was still Peter Dixon, Peter Wheeler and myself who were all more experienced as players and leaders. It was also surprising because Billy was such a shy, reserved sort of guy. I can remember him when he first came into the Lancashire team — he wouldn't say boo to a goose. Then he was the same with England. But as in everything he did he developed."

Even though there was much surprise at the decisions there was no resentment, for Billy was always respected as

Bill Beaumont and Steve Smith dispute a loose ball.

Beaumont on the charge against Scotland. (1980)

an honest man and a good player. He in turn relied heavily on the advice of his more experienced colleagues in the early days. In paying tribute to them he would have you believe that he really had nothing to do except play because the rest of the side made it easy for him.

However naïve he was at the beginning he was obviously a quick learner, because when Uttley reappeared at the beginning of the 1980 season, having again been sidelined for a lengthy spell with that troublesome back injury, there was no question of reinstating him as captain.

Second row is not the best place in the team to captain from. For long periods you have your head buried in the scrum and when you do emerge you have to react immediately to the play, so there is little time to stand back and make a cool appraisal of the situation. Therefore most forward captains have made their names as motivators. Willie John McBride is the classic example. His men would follow him anywhere, but with his natural shyness Billy Beaumont was not ideally suited to that role. Yet he achieved the same sort of response, and the concern of the players at having to play without him when he retired was totally genuine.

Fran Cotton thinks it was because "He was such a genuine honest sort of bloke. You often get captains who say all the right things, but with Billy you knew he would be the first to try and carry them out. If you see him trying that hard you've got to give him a bit more yourself." Steve Smith, who succeeded him as captain, endorses that and recalls how hard he worked at captaincy, particularly when England were on tour: "He would never take time off, even when we were all having fun — and Billy enjoys a

Beaumont chaired by Fran Cotton after the Grand Slam game against Scotland in 1980.

beer as much as the next guy — he was still aware of his duties. He lived the part and was always looking after the other players." Both agree that he was not a great man on the tactical side, although by the end of his career he had a much fuller appreciation of that side of the job. Again it was his ability to learn and learn quickly that impressed his fellow players. Steve Smith again: "There's no doubt that he was given the captaincy too early, that wasn't his fault — and would you turn it down? But in the early days he was very reliant on Franny and Nero (Tony Neary). When they went he didn't even miss them."

This determination and ability to learn quickly also stood him in good stead as he developed as a player. At school he was a full back and continued to play in that position even though he had grown to 6'3" and weighed almost 17 stone when he joined Fylde. He was a good squash player, cricketer and golfer, which probably explains why he was a much better ball-player than most second rows and why his handling was always so sure. Playing alongside him so often, Steve Smith also noticed other bonuses not usually expected from a second row: "If he peeled from a lineout he wouldn't automatically put his head down and close his eyes. At times he would straighten a man up and give the ball at exactly the right moment, a thing even the backs find difficult these days; he even sold the odd dummy. He was also quicker than the average second row. Like all big men he took time to get up a head of steam but would often beat some of the backs in a long sprint in training. He would always be the fourth man to the ball in a match. None of the rest of the front five ever beat him to it."

Smithy obviously has enormous admiration for him as a man and a player but is always the first to take the opportunity to laugh at the Beaumont backside. He sums him up with: "You're too intelligent to be a second row but you can't play anywhere else with a shape like that." That might be a case of the pot calling the kettle black but he was soon proved correct at Fylde, and from the sixth team full back Beaumont progressed within two years to first team second row.

That was in 1972, and from then on his progress was spectacular. In 1973 he was on the substitutes bench for England U 23 against Tonga, and in 1975 he won his first cap. In 1977 he was called out as a replacement for the Lions tour to New Zealand and immediately threw himself into the fray with such commitment that he proved the original selection wrong by playing in the last three Tests. It was not a happy tour but Beaumont was one of the few players who came out of it with nothing but credit.

In the 1980 domestic season he achieved everything but victory over New Zealand with the England side. He captained the North when they beat the tourists, captained Lancashire to the County Championship, and skippered England to their first Grand Slam for 23 years. Quite naturally he was everyone's choice as "Player of the Year", and the obvious selection to captain the Lions.

Beaumont leaves the field for the last time during the Lancs./N. Midlands County Championships Final 1982.

A fine pair.

Although they did not win the series he made a great personal success of that too. In doing so he earned the lasting respect of the players of the other home countries as a captain and a player.

John Dawes, his coach in 1977, was lavish in his praise for Beaumont the tourist, and thought the way that he fought his way into the Test team in New Zealand was magnificent. Derek Quinnell still recalls the way he worked at his game during the tour. "I didn't rate him as a lineout jumper initially but after every practice session he would stay out on the park with Peter Wheeler, long after the rest of us had gone in, to improve his technique. By the end of the tour he could handle anything the All Blacks could throw at him."

Gentleman Bill in the stand.

The Beaumont backside certainly seems to be his most important asset as far as his fellow players are concerned. It had its most famous moment when Erica Roe took the field in what turned out to be Billy's last but one international. There he was giving his half-time exhortation to his team when it became obvious that he was not commanding their full attention. As the noise from the crowd grew to a deafening roar he was at last distracted from his theme and asked what was going on. Peter Wheeler had the answer: "There's a bloke running around on the pitch with your arse on his chest." Even Billy gave up as the whole team collapsed in laughter.

Cliff Morgan was very fond of tapping his head and then his ankles and saying, "Up here for thinking down there for dancing". Billy's version would have been "Up here for thinking down there for pushing". One thing though is for certain, as England found out when they had to play out the rest of the international season without him: his brains certainly were not in his backside.

7
MISSED CHANCES

David Duckham

To the more discerning observer, not to mention the players themselves, England's international season of 1981/82 will doubtless offer the almost inevitable and certainly frustrating poser as to what might have been. A disappointing stalemate against Scotland, an undignified defeat at the hands of Ireland, but then a heartwarming recovery in Paris, followed by a conclusive victory over Wales at Twickenham. If only . . .

It is worth remembering that the recall in 1977 of Sandy Sanders to chair the England Selection Committee, together with the simultaneous call-up to its ranks of Budge Rogers, had been regarded by many as the turning point in the fortunes of the national team, following a decade in the shadows. Sanders himself deserved much of the credit for restoring a sense of pride to the England camp. Rogers injected some much-needed realism when he was subsequently elected to the chair, and a renewed feeling of self-assurance was generated amongst the players. Mike Davis became coach and these two, whose relationship with the squad was closer than that of any of their predecessors, pioneered a much-needed recovery. A new slim-line Steve Smith appeared to improve co-ordination. The strength of Phil Blakeway at prop secured the scrum, and Bill Beaumont emerged as a magnificent leader. The result: a well-deserved Grand Slam in 1980.

Last season, however, even as reigning champions for

the first time since 1963, England's performance was mixed, though second place in the Championship Table was hardly a disaster after the huge success of a year earlier.

Previous forward power had not been fully exploited behind the scrum but Messrs Neary, Uttley and Cotton were now absent and the three-quarters developed into a most effective unit. Huw Davies and Marcus Rose added youthful flair alongside the much improved Leicester pairing of Clive Woodward and Paul Dodge, while John Carleton and Mike Slemen hovered on the wings. It was an ironic change of emphasis following several years of forward strength.

And so to the 1981/82 season, which provided an additional challenge from the touring Australians. With hindsight, international form against the Wallabies was hardly an accurate pointer to the outcome of the Championship, considering that Ireland eventually secured the Triple Crown after being the only Australian scalp. Nevertheless, on January 2nd England performed creditably, despite the fact that the majority of the team had played little rugby during December because of the harsh weather. Even so, it was the loss of the concussed Mike Slemen late in the first half that provided some real inspiration for Nick Jeavons' try near the posts when the side was temporarily reduced to fourteen men. This was a crucial psychological moment for the England players, and one from which they never looked back. After an indifferent opening during which a number of Australian attacks had all but succeeded, Mark Ella, the Wallabies' talented fly-half, elected to run from under his own posts and was unceremoniously tackled in possession. From that position, England set up Jeavons to drive through Ella's tackle for the vital score. The 15-11 victory was not entirely convincing, although one calculated gamble by Budge Rogers did pay off. Peter Winterbottom, a young Headingley flanker, more than justified his first cap with a vigorously mobile performance. A meteoric rise to prominence for one so inexperienced; yet his style and commitment was more than reminiscent of an equally impressive debut by Jean-Pierre Rives at Twickenham in 1975.

Player confidence was considerably enhanced during the preparations for the first hurdle of the Championship twelve days later against Scotland at Murrayfield, the scene of the Grand Slam two years before. A distinctly haphazard build-up to the game with Australia — a legacy of the extreme weather conditions — was now history, and Skipper Bill Beaumont could at least look forward to the threat across the Border with renewed vigour. The Scots, eminently dangerous behind the scrum but lacking England's total solidity up front, refused to be taken

Carleton tackled by Kiernan with Winterbottom in support.

Maurice Colclough feeds
Steve Smith.

lightly as the match unfolded. England's young back-row combination, in need of greater creativity to complement the proven ball-winning skills of the revised front five, managed to hold their more experienced counterparts in a series of scrappy exchanges. Missing was the control and sheer physical presence of John Scott, out of action this far because of operations on both ankles. Even so, Bob Hesford of Bristol proved an able deputy and did all that was asked of him. Both sides believed their strength to be close to the protective blanket of their forwards and the outcome was, as one learned journal wrote afterwards, "No tries and a set of appallingly negative statistics".

Indeed, the honours were even in most phases, and there was little to enthuse over in the way of individual flair. England in fact were still leading in the fourth minute of injury time when prop Colin Smart foolishly shoulder-charged Ian Paxton off the ball barely inside England's half and Andy Irvine drew the match with a beautifully struck kick. The closing stages had been agonisingly tense and exciting, yet the score line had remained unaltered throughout the half. During the first period Rutherford's early drop goal had been eventually matched by a Dodge penalty following three missed chances by Rose. Irvine was soon on target when Woodward obstructed, but Dodge replied again and then Rose took the lead with a simple penalty almost on half-time. Despite Irvine's failure to convert two further chances, Scottish pressure was finally rewarded. A dramatic climax to a contest blurred by tension and largely neutralised by lack of imagination.

For the next encounter against Ireland at Twickenham, Budge Rogers succumbed to the temptation of replacing Hesford with a half-fit Scott. Hesford was, perhaps, the victim of an element of desperation on the Selectors' part, but the calculated reasoning behind the change was quite obvious to all and sundry. With that said, Rogers could not possibly have foreseen the ensuing drama, for Beaumont was forced to withdraw on medical advice arising from the aggravation of an old head injury which had caused his premature departure in the County Championship Final on January 30th, just seven days before the Irish match. It was a mortifying blow, over-shadowing the subsequent eleventh-hour cry-off by Paul Dodge, who pulled a hamstring in training. His replacement by Tony Bond, whose forthright aggression both in attack and defence would complement Woodward's skills, was a sensible move, albeit the only realistic option available. John Syddall of Waterloo faced the unenviable task of deputising for Beaumont and the leadership was handed to Steve Smith who, for his experience and undeniable charisma, might well have been the players' choice. In short, a man to respect, even in the wake of his eminent predecessor.

England's showing in the eighty minutes that followed would, from my own conservative stand-point, be best described as unmemorable, on the basis that the sooner it was forgotten the better. Ireland's triumph by a single point hardly did credit to the endeavour and spirit shown by Ciaran Fitzgerald and his men, who suppressed their totally unconvincing opponents. Justice was seen to be done when, after McLoughlin had been driven over the line by what seemed to be the majority of the Irish team, Ollie Campbell kicked an incredible conversion across a stiff breeze and from the most difficult of angles. England simply could not withstand the relentless pressure exerted by the visitors. For their part, the Irishmen did not simply spoil English possession, as had been feared, but positively benefited from it. England's scrummaging power was successfully countered, and behind, Ireland's defence was unflinching. In addition Campbell, already the architect of Wales' downfall in Dublin, gave a truly breathtaking display. Even Smith's courageous charge-down of his attempted drop goal led to McLoughlin's try! Ireland led at the interval by 10-3: a try by MacNeill and two Campbell penalties against a solitary effort from Rose who had already missed with two other long-range

Mike Slemen scores for England against Ireland.

Huw Davies playing for Cambridge.

attempts. He subsequently added two more, either side of the other Irish try, and in injury time converted a consolation try by Slemen.

Suddenly, questions were being asked about England's future in the Championship. I, amongst others, went as far as to suggest in a newspaper column that the team had taken a regressive step towards the depression of the previous decade, when resistance had stagnated at a particularly low ebb. Notwithstanding the absence of their illustrious leader, who was no doubt a considerable source of inspiration, the team had lacked both the confidence and the ability to remain calm under intense pressure. Play was both disorganised and incoherent.

Dusty Hares converts a
first half penalty against
France.

Furthermore, handling mistakes and other errors of judgement were in abundance. Even Mike Slemen was uncharacteristically at fault on more than one occasion. Huw Davies had an uneasy afternoon, although he did fashion Slemen's try almost out of nothing. Marcus Rose apparently does nothing by halves, for he was either brilliant or guilty of a disastrous error. With that unfailing wisdom of hindsight once again, Budge Rogers almost certainly erred in the premature reinstatement of Scott who, whilst controlling the base of the scrum and in doing so generating three points for an off-side decision, overdid the delayed heel and was a mere shadow of himself in the lineout.

Having conclusively proved Rogers to be at fault after the event, I committed myself in print, before the team to meet France was announced, with a plea to the Selectors to resist further changes. *The Times* evidently does not feature amongst their reading material because both Rose

Paul Dodge breaks with Clive Woodward in support.

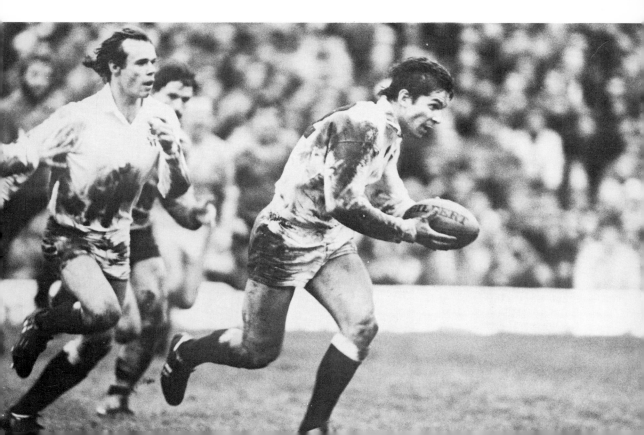

Steve Smith, the
England captain, clears
his lines watched by
Carpentier (France) and
Bainbridge.

and Davies lost their places, to Dusty Hare and Les Cusworth respectively. Predictably, Paul Dodge was restored for his mid-field poise, and it was inevitable that Beaumont would also return. With that said, readers will hardly need reminding of the tragedy of Beaumont's wise decision to retire before the French match with the benefit of extensive medical counsel. Surely his contribution to English rugby as a player is immeasurable.

Whilst I still maintain that Rose and Davies will prove better long-term prospects at international level, the resurrection of Hare and Cusworth was arguably justified on the basis that the former was more consistently dependable in the kicking stakes, whereas the latter would inject greater stability behind the scrum. Also, the superb efficiency of the highly talented Leicester three-quarter line was now being fully recognised. Whatever had been the final combination to take on France at the imposing Parc des Prince Stadium, it would not have escaped the notice of Smith and co that they were now confronted with two nations who historically had both proved the most difficult of European opponents.

On February 20th a huge contingent of English supporters witnessed a heartwarming display which comprehensively disproved a widely held view (supported unfortunately by an ominous array of statistics) that the French team were about to erect another English tombstone. A proliferation of previous England debacles across the water, notwithstanding the prevailing eccentricity of the French Selectors (motto: *if in doubt, panic*), was never likely to instigate a feeling of nationwide security. Even Hare himself must have been at least vaguely conscious of the fate which had befallen several of his predecessors. On the other hand, such was the measure of England's victory (27-15) that the vagaries of previous encounters in Paris might well have served to redouble player resolve in the quest for success and the restoration of a lasting credibility.

Marcus Rose kicks as
Bob Hesford looks on.

The final score was a little flattering, yet the French players, young and inexperienced, seemed resolved to embark upon a game of roulette with the referee and consequently paid a heavy price. Nevertheless, sparks of their inherently brilliant individualism were occasionally in evidence and certainly contributed to their solitary try, when Hare was wrong-footed with alarming ease by his opposite number Sallefranque to give Pardo the touchdown. Lescaboura dropped an astonishing goal from fully fifty yards to remind the English ensemble of how Gallic flair can express itself when allowed to. The other French points all came from his boot. How sad it was that much of the Tricolours' initiative was so desperately disjointed.

From England's point of view the memory of avoidable errors and a rather ponderous forward display against Ireland was firmly banished. The most significant feature of the play was the form of Dusty Hare, whose heroic contribution of nineteen points provided the essential difference between the two teams. In my view his

Steve Smith passes back.

performance was not simply faultless, embodying character and unflappable verve, but quite probably his finest during a spasmodic international career. Yet, for all his virtuosity, it should be remembered that *Lady Luck* herself had intervened to resurrect him from apparent oblivion. He was selected after the withdrawal of Nick Stringer, who was originally chosen to displace Marcus Rose. However, Stringer withdrew after not recovering from an injury he sustained on his debut when he replaced Mike Slemen against Australia. Slemen demonstrated his immense shrewdness by catching the French defence completely unawares when he took a quick drop-out downfield, gave chase and then allowed himself to be outrun by the faithfully supporting Woodward who dribbled on to score a spectacular try near the posts. Not to be outdone, John Carleton weaved his way over near the final whistle after an intuitive blind-side break by Smith and a surprisingly well-timed pass from Colin Smart. England were back in business.

Only the formidable challenge of Wales (whose own special brand of brilliance had already been on view against France) remained to question England's recovery and at least a modest placing in the Championship Table. An unchanged line-up took to the field at Twickenham on March 6th and earned an emphatic win to dilute a disastrous run against the old enemy during the previous twenty years. The try count of two to one may have convinced even the more passionate Welsh supporters that England's victory was well-deserved. Granted, the loss of Terry Holmes with a shoulder injury shortly after half-time was a cruel blow to the visitors, who could make little headway thereafter. The whole of the Principality had pinned their faith on Holmes but he was not there to lead what turned out to be a patchy assault on an 11 point deficit. If anything, English resolve strengthened, apparently unmindful of Wales' recovery at Twickenham twelve years earlier when Ray Hopkins, having already replaced the injured Gareth Edwards to win his solitary

John Carleton beats Clive Rees for his try.

John Scott
acknowledges cheers as
he captains Cardiff to a
very narrow victory over
Bridgend — Welsh Cup
Final 1982.

cap, spearheaded a startling offensive which transformed a 3-13 disadvantage into a 17-13 victory.

On the day, England's early initiative and refreshing enterprise was suitably rewarded. Slemen (equalling Peter Squires' record of 29 caps on the wing) opened the scoring after a series of well-worked attacks downfield. Hare missed the conversion and two earlier penalties. He later atoned and then Carleton produced the highlight of the match. Intelligently deputising for his captain, Smith, who was buried in a ruck, seized the loose ball, spotted a gap in the Welsh defence and proceeded to out-sprint Holmes, Rees and Evans to the line without a finger being laid on him. Hare again missed a kickable conversion but added another penalty which concluded the scoring. By then it was all over.

At the end of the day Welsh skipper, Gareth Davies, might have regretted his decision to face a swirling breeze during the first half. Even the seven point deficit at half-time was not insurmountable, but a response from the

Welsh team did not materialise and a discernible measure of desperation was easily countered by a resolute English defence. The English performance was highly commendable but not completely without blemish. Dodge, for example, normally very dependable, was guilty of allowing the elusive Donovan to escape his clutches more than once. Donovan in fact was the only Welsh back on view who looked capable of an incisive break. It was particularly gratifying nevertheless that, after a fiercely devious opening against Scotland and Ireland, the team completed the season on the highest of notes.

Though inconceivable at the outset, the eventual recall of Hare and Cusworth was more than justified. Hare

Gloucester v. Moseley in the John Player Cup Final 1982.

proved his worth in Paris whereas Cusworth, the most adventurous of runners, managed to inject a reviving breadth to the three-quarter play, aided no doubt by a precious understanding with his club colleagues, Dodge and Woodward. The departure of Beaumont, initially considered a major hiccup in England's plans, was well compensated by the endearing character of Steve Smith, who shouldered his responsibility with much aplomb and composure. It was fitting that he should celebrate the victory over Wales by eclipsing Dick Jeeps' long-standing record tally of caps at scrum-half.

At the time of writing the 1982/83 campaign seems a distant prospect, yet one feels reasonably secure in the knowledge that Messrs Rogers and Davis will already be planning ahead. The England tour to North America will soon be underway, and whilst a number of notable personnel will be absent for various reasons, the opportunity is there to re-establish and consolidate the depth of talent within the squad. Furthmore, I fancy that S. J. Smith Esq. will not be in too great a hurry to relinquish his well-earned captaincy.

8
SOSPAN FAWR

Derek Quinnell

Two miles down the road from where I was born stands
Stradey Park, and for the entire eighteen years of my playing career the only club I played for, except for
representative games, was Llanelli Rugby Football Club.
In fact, I owe my success in the game, and more importantly my enthusiasm for it to some wise men at
Stradey Park, but more of that later.

When I was three years old I "emigrated"; about five
miles up the B4308 road, to Trimsaran. It was there, or
more precisely in "Cae James" — Farmer James' field —
that I first put boot and hand to ball. Since there was no
playing field at Trimsaran Primary, "Cae James" provided us with the nearest equivalent to a real rugby
ground. My education brought me back to the rugby
Mecca when I entered Coleshill Secondary Modern
School, and it was at the age of eleven that I first took part
in any form of organised rugby. The cries of "Where do I
stand, sir?" were quite common, unlike today when,
sadly, many a nine or ten year-old is already an embittered
campaigner for some under-11 team or another. I think,
too, that our games in "Cae James" were important in
that it was us, the kids, charging up and down the pitch
and probably breaking every rule in the official W.R.U.
Handbook, who were playing. There was no watchful or
over-eager parental eye following the game. The tactics
were confined to "whoever had the ball ran!"

Coleshill School, bang in the middle of Llanelli, overlooked by the Town Hall, provided me with my first tuition in rugby. Former Llanelli full back Mervyn Bowen guided me and the many novices in the first rudiments of rugby. In my class for the first two years I often had to sit beside Phil Bennett. He also had a slight penchant for the game! And it was in the very first years of the sixties that I had my first taste of competitive rugby, and some inkling that Phil Bennett was to be a star of the future. Benny and I were chosen to play for the Llanelli Schools and reached the final of the Dewar Shield Cup, only to lose to Bridgend Schools. After that game Benny and I parted company. He went off to play for Felinfoel youth. Felinfoel is famous now, of course, for Benny and its beer (in that order!).

It did not seem long before I was in the Llanelli Youth Team. Llanelli Youth is a junior side of Llanelli R.F.C. and thus with my first game in 1964 I started my link with Stradey, and ever since have been a confirmed *sospan*!

It might seem strange, looking back to that year and the pride I felt in actually playing for the Youth team, that I had no real ambition or even the slightest idea that international status was beckoning. I never had the burning ambition to don the Welsh Jersey when I was thirteen or fourteen. My aims and targets were limited to the possibility of playing for the next best team, the under-13s, then the under-15s, and so on.

It was in my first year as a Llanelli Youth player that I was given my first trial in the Welsh Youth Team. Although I played at No. 8 in the Llanelli Youth side, I received all my Welsh Youth caps as a second row forward. One of my proudest moments in those days was when we actually beat the French Youth for the first time in history on French soil. That was a major breakthrough for Welsh rugby. In the same season, I played my first game for the Senior Llanelli team. I had arrived!

As I mentioned earlier, the wisdom of some Llanelli Selectors was shown in the manner in which a new young player was introduced into the senior team. My first game was a Christmas fixture, which in itself meant that no-one was going to be playing flat out. Moreover, it was not against Swansea or Cardiff but against the University Athletics Union, which meant that I was playing against a team containing considerably more youthful players than the average South Wales team. In addition, a new cap was limited to only six games for the senior team in his year of initiation, and of the five games I played in that 1967/68 season never once was I picked to oppose a hardened and experienced team.

However, I was shown that it was not all "wine and roses". The very last game for Llanelli of that season was against Neath at the Gnoll ground, and victory in this match would clinch the *Western Mail* unofficial Championship. I was asked to attend as a possible player, but more probably as a reserve. As it turned out, I was very glad I was not picked. The adrenalin was pumping, and the feeling of unease was quite marked. Neath, led by a ferocious pack with Brian Thomas as commander,

Delme Thomas in action during a lineout.

A word of advice from Delme.

proved a formidable opposition. The game was won, but not before my brother-in-law, Alan John, left the field with a broken collar bone, and Marsden Morgan had his nose so badly broken that he could see out of only one eye; not because of the swelling but because his nose was covering it. Bert Peel, the Llanelli trainer, pronounced it simply a bad bruising! It was in that game that Stuart Gallagher was also injured but bravely made up the numbers to stem the All Black tide for most of the proceedings. All that I can say is, thank the Lord the new substitute rule had not come into force!

But even if I never appeared for the Scarlets in any of the big games, it was a tremendous experience to have been part of the squad in that Championship year. As it happened, because of Stuart Gallagher's injury, I was picked to play at the Welsh Sevens on the following Saturday, and Llanelli carried off the cup. Again, at the start of the new season 1968/69, I was chosen to play for the Scarlets in the Snelling Sevens, but alas we lost to

Cardiff in the final. The referee, incidently, was Gwynne Walters, now a revered Llanelli committee man. For some unknown reason, though every other half was ten minutes long, the second half in the final was fourteen minutes, and the last act in the dying seconds of the fourteenth minute was performed by Billy Hullin as he dived into the corner to give Cardiff the lead and subsequent victory. Gwynne, we have forgiven but not forgotten! Somebody mentioned injury time but *I* can't remember any injuries.

It was in 1968/69 that I played my first full season at Stradey, and whilst the team contained great names such as Delme Thomas and Norman Gale, a new crop of first-class players were being created. Phil Bennett, Alan and Clive John in my first year, and later Ray Gravell, Hefin and Gareth Jenkins, Roy Bergiers and many more. To play one's first full season alongside such newcomers was quite inspiring. They formed a nucleus of the side that went on to achieve great success. I should also mention that in those early years Bert Peel, who joined as youth trainer in the same year as I began playing for Llanelli

Passing back.

Youth, was a key force. He was the trainer and physio for the team by the time I gained my place and became a very good friend. He was a great character and will always be missed.

My next season saw the arrival of the Springboks, and I thought we were very unlucky to lose to them 10-9. Due to Welsh commitments we lost the services of both Phil Bennett (playing on the wing for Wales) and Delme Thomas. The try we scored against the Boks that day was even greater, in my opinion, than the famous Barbarian try against the All Blacks in 1973. Almost every player in the Llanelli side handled that ball, some even twice, before another old classmate from Coleshill, Alan Richards, scored in the corner. It was a truly marvellous performance from such a young side, and it was that game that really made me feel that I had "arrived" in first-class rugby. I had to mark Frik du Preez at the front of the line-out, and having played against that huge Springbok pack and held my own, I knew that I could play against any pack in the world.

The following Saturday I was sitting on the Welsh bench for the first time. In fact I spent two years and ten matches on the bench before I gained my first cap! But when one considers that at that time the No. 8 spot was held by Mervyn Davies, and that the two second row places were being contested by Geoff Evans and Mike Roberts of London Welsh, Delme Thomas, Alan Martin, and myself, it is not difficult to understand how hard the competition was. At that time, of course, although I had played a few games as a flanker for Llanelli, and at that position in a Welsh trial at Pontypool, I was not seriously considered as an international wing forward. In any event, there were a few flankers around with names like John Taylor and Dai Morris. I should also not forget to mention, for modesty's sake, the terrible defeat the Barbarians suffered against the Fijians at Gosforth in 1970 — I was wing forward for that game too!

However, I did eventually get a cap in the No. 6 shirt

for the Lions tour of New Zealand in 1971. That tour was probably the most exhilarating rugby experience in my playing career. The All Black pack consisted of very large men, and their wing forwards were no exception. Consequently, with Mervyn Davies at No. 8 for all the important games (he was the only genuine No. 8 selected for the tour) I was chosen as a blind side wing forward. In the lesser games, Peter Dixon and I filled in at the back of the scrum. It was essential that a large blind side flanker was selected to compensate for and add alternative play to the "flyers", the high speed open side players, John Taylor, Fergus Slattery and Mike Hipwell. In some games, such as the infamous Canterbury match I was not picked, and I felt a couple of larger players might have helped. Barry John was quite pleased to be on the bench next to me! Understandably, so I suppose, but I found it very frustrating only being able to shout and not get physically involved with the game.

On the whole, the way the game was played in New Zealand suited me better than in South Africa or Europe. Generally, the All Blacks played a much tighter game, and thus one played close to the scrum; being my size this style of play came a lot easier. My favourite position was still No. 8, since it was really a cross between second row and flank forward. Second row play is grafting all the time, whereas at flanker one is expected to fly around continuously. Well, I've never been keen on too much grafting or too much flying, so if one had to play, No. 8 was the best since we didn't have to do too much of either!

But as I mentioned, my first representative cap was donned for the Lions in the Third Test of the 1971 tour. It was the only Test I played in, since Peter Dixon and John Taylor gained the positions alongside Mervyn in the first two Tests. It was an extremely important game for the tour since the scoresheet was one-all, and if this match resulted in victory for the Lions, then we couldn't lose the series. We won the game, but alas I suffered an injury and subsequently was ineligible for selection in the Fourth Test.

Get off my back!

I look back on that win with good memories. There was tremendous team spirit and in Doug Smith and Carwyn James we had top class management. Doug Smith was marvellous at keeping the players free from off-field pressures. He committed us rightly to our fair share of public relations work, but it was always he who carried the ultimate pressures that inevitably arise on a long tour. Carwyn on the lines was the force on the field, and it was he who named me "Sloppy" after a very uninspiring training session. You might have heard of King John, but I was Sloppy Quinnell!

What was so good about Doug and Carwyn was that each complemented the other while at the same time helping in each other's so-called "defined duties". It was really Doug's job to liaise with the press, but I remember staying at one hotel in which my room was directly above Carwyn's. On coming back very late one evening, I noticed Carwyn's light was still on — he was giving an impromptu press meeting. So, when he did eventually name me Sloppy, I told him it was because he kept me up so late at his all-night party.

Likewise, Doug Smith would help out on the training field. Carwyn used to put Doug's ample sixteen-and-a-half stone frame to good use by making players carry him around the park if they committed any misdemeanour. The lads only had to do this once and then they gave Carwyn their full attention.

Both Doug's and Carwyn's ability to get on with people, and more particularly with the press, led to the 1971 tour being a very happy one, and I am sure this was one of the important factors in the success of the tour. Unfortunately, in 1977 the tour management and the press were at loggerheads, and whilst one could understand their contrasting views, it was difficult to be disloyal to the management of a touring party and at the same time be discourteous to the host nation's press. The Lions tour should be seen as a flag-carrying exercise not a sword-bearing campaign. This was well displayed by both

Sid Miller and Noel Murphy on the 1980 tour of South Africa, another genuinely happy tour.

The season following our tour of 1971 brought me my first Welsh cap. I was on the bench (again!) for the 1972 match against France at Cardiff. It was a great experience, as I think the television cameras have so often shown. I would like at this late stage publicly to congratulate the referee, Mike Titcombe, for keeping the game alive for so long that I had time to get on to the Cardiff Arms Park. I am sure that if he had played another minute of extra time I would have dropped a goal; for it has always been my ambition to drop a goal for Wales. I should also mention that I've since bought a lot of beer for Mervyn, who came off to let me on!

The feeling of running on to that pitch for the first time can never come back — one is so charged with emotion, the senses are aflame. In fact, on that day I was halfway across the field before I realised I was still sucking a Fox's Glacier Fruit. My mother told me I should have been ashamed of myself for spitting in front of the television cameras and all those millions of people.

At the end of that game I got into the Welsh team bath for the very first time with dirty knees and not straight out of a tracksuit. But there was plenty of bench sitting to come. I won another eight caps but only after another four seasons of international rugby.

I have often been asked whether during this period I was disappointed not to have gone on the most successful Lions tour of all times, the 1974 tour of South Africa. Obviously, it would have been a great privilege to have gone and to have been part of a team so highly lauded, but no, I was not disappointed.

However, I was back touring in 1976. Wales selected the first ever European team to take on Japan. The Japanese were the warmest hosts one could wish for, and although the scores against the Japanese teams were always high, the games were not as easy as the results suggested. I have seen many a tennis game played when one player eventually wins 6-0, 6-1, 6-1. The figures often have never reflected the real game. It was so with Japan. The games were very hard, and even though there was an advantage in height and size, generally there always seemed to be three players to contend with the covering was so good. Another great fact in the Japanese game was their tackling - it was always low and hard and it's true what they say, when the bigger men fall, they fall harder. Two or three Japanese tackling coaches wouldn't go amiss in Europe.

The greatest game I played in for Wales must have been our victory over Ireland in Dublin in 1978, when Wales won the Triple Crown. It was Gareth Edwards' last game and was a fitting tribute to so great a player. I was playing in my favourite position, No. 8, but remember having a particularly hard game. In fact, it was probably the hardest game I ever took part in. Willie Duggan, a great player and friend, was quite tremendous for Ireland on that day and often I wished he was on our side.

At the end of that season we all confidently went off to Australia in the hope of conquering the Wallabies. People will always regard it as the "infamous" tour; the one in which Graham Price had his jaw broken, the tour where all Welshmen were at loggerheads with the Aussies and their press. But to be honest, it was a very enjoyable tour and an interesting and happy experience. The management of Clive Rowlands and John Dawes created a fine ambience in which the players could relax. The press relationship, despite what many people heard, was friendly and co-operative. It was, I am sure, a very good thing for the tour that the inexcusable attack on Graham Price occurred in the last game of the tour, as this would have soured all the tour had it happened earlier. But I would like to emphasise that the trip was not the battle-field so often reported.

Looking back at my own career, rugby has given me the all important advantage of meeting hundreds of people, thousands of miles apart and from different cultures,

Bennie on the break.

races and environments. I have travelled twice round the world with rugby teams, something that would, for me, have been impossible were it not for the game.

At the end of the season such as the last, which has seen the senior Welsh side losing three of its four internationals in the Home Championship and its home ground record, it is not surprising that the Welsh Rugby Union have set up a committee to analyse the state of Welsh rugby. This committee, under the chairmanship of Ieuan Evans, has a brief to look into all aspects of the game, and it's worth looking at some of the points causing most concern.

The best place to start is at the beginning, the first stage of rugby — the under-11s group. My eldest son started playing rugby for the Llanelli under-11s B side when he was two months into his ninth year. I genuinely feel it was too early, but boys are now so enthusiastic to emulate the players they see on television that eventually I agreed to let him start his rugby career. The first game in which he played was against Bridgend under-11s and it was with some trepidation that I phoned home from Ireland, where I had been playing for Llanelli against Leinster, not so much to know the result as to check whether he was still in one piece and unharmed. I had told him to be ready for the call, and when I asked him how he had got on his immediate reply was, "We had a great pie and chips after the game, and fantastic apple tart and cream." He'd enjoyed himself, obviously. He mentioned as an afterthought that they had been well and truly beaten! The one thing that I didn't want my boy or any other kid playing at that level to believe is that winning is the all important essence of rugby football. It is essential

Gravell scoring for Llanelli.

that coaches and teachers ensure that the lads learn the basic skills of taking and giving the ball and of running freely. At this stage, the youngsters' flair should not be stifled, and they should be left their freedom to do their "own thing" within a loose framework of the laws. Any parent on the touchline who wants his ten year-old son to out-scrummage the opposing prop should be made to prop against Graham Price in twenty scrums at a Welsh squad training session one Sunday afternoon. Attitudes might change in those circumstances.

At this early stage no real emphasis should be put on any form of highly disciplined rugby, and no genuine competitive matches should be entered into. By the time the boys are fourteen they should have a knowledge of the laws of the game, and should be beginning to find positions which they and their teachers think the most suitable. At this stage they see themselves as budding Edwards, Bennetts or Martins, and consequently they become aware of what the senior players are doing in their positions. Some of us at senior level often forget that in the crowd are youngsters watching the game who will not take their eyes off the play for the full eighty minutes because they want to copy every move in their own team game the next week. Some of us may have a lot to answer for, and if we had all given a thought to those lads before taking the field the game might be a little better for it.

It is worthwhile remembering that the game is best when it is kept simple, and this applies to all levels. At a young age, it is vital that one is kept involved in the game, otherwise the budding young wings, who never gets the ball, will soon take to some other sport for enjoyment. When the 1971 Lions met recently to make a television film, it was tremendous to see the old clips from the tour, to see all the wings getting a hat-full of tries, simply because the game was kept simple and the ball was moved swiftly down the wings. We have to encourage our children to do the same.

The years between 15 and 19 are perhaps the most important years of all. Having graduated to senior school sides, or if out of school to a youth or Colts team, the next step is the "big-time". Whether it's for a college, Llanelli Wanderers' seconds, or for one of the first-class sides depends very much on these 15-19 year olds. Some boys are already as tall as ever they will be by the time they reach the age of 15. I well remember a lad in my own village who was great at the under-11 stage and a star as a schoolboy player but who, by the time he had reached youth level, had had enough of the game, and now at 20 has not played for over five years.

It is vital to nurture these young players and to make sure that neither their bodies nor their minds are over-spent. By the time they are reaching the end of their senior school or youth rugby they are 90 per cent developed rugby players in the sense that they have developed most of their strength, stamina and speed. Over the next two or three years the finishing touches will be added to all

Derek Quinnell.

their important attributes. But it must be remembered that they will still be developing as players in senior rugby; forwards are still developing in their early 20s.

It is, I feel, as important to keep senior players "fresh" as it is to keep young boys unfettered by tactics, team talks and complicated coaching. It just has to be said that nowadays there is far too much rugby at senior club level; to look at many of the fixture lists one would think that some of these teams play all the year round. There are so many games these days for senior players to compete in that there is little time for training. If rugby players are not training they cannot be fully fit, and if they're not fully fit they cannot play to the best of their ability. I would advocate a drastic reduction in the number of games by these top 16 Welsh clubs. New Zealand, it has been said by one eminent rugby writer, is the only country still to keep playing attractive rugby at a top class level, and their fixture lists are considerably shorter than ours. Playing, I know, is more fun than training, but an essential part of any physical sport is fitness and we must give our top players more time to stay fit.

9
WAKA'S MEN

Don Cameron

The All Blacks of the Graham Mourie era have, these last five years, been such regular visitors to Europe they have almost worn a rut in the rugby road. Since 1977 Mourie's men have been twice to France, twice to Italy, once to Romania, taken in the British Isles with the Grand Slam tour of 1978, visited England and Scotland in 1979, and then participated in the grandeur of the Welsh centenary celebrations of 1980.

Rugby is a game of so many flickering colours that such a routine procession of tours can never be dull, but nevertheless it is time for a change, for a glimpse beneath the hard shell of the All Black aura, for a hint at what lies at the heart of New Zealand rugby.

The New Zealand Maoris, who will play seven matches in Wales in October and November — the last against a Welsh XV at the beloved Arms Park which all New Zealand will regard as a special "test" — will provide that glimpse, that touch of a fascinating aspect of New Zealand rugby left dormant for so long.

From the time, many months ago, when the Maoris' tour was arranged, there has been a heady undercurrent rippling through New Zealand rugby. You only needed to spend an hour in the company of leading Maori players before the magic words came out: "We are going to Wales." A flash in the eye, a spring in the step . . . what a marvellous tour it will be — a meeting of two peoples with a special affinity for the game.

For, even with the handicap of looking at Maori rugby through a Pakeha's eyes, I feel that among the rugby people of the world the Welsh and the Maoris are the closest brothers in the game. New Zealanders as a whole pride themselves in their affection for rugby, and their ability to play the game. But New Zealanders are really an unemotional lot in that they do not readily let their emotions flood out. There is still some of the English stiff upper lip left in the national rugby psyche.

They have rugby in their hearts, but do they have it in their passions? The Welsh do. And so, bless them, have the Maoris.

There is the oft-used saying that when the British colonised many parts of the world they brought with them two great achievements — the limited liability company and the game of cricket. To New Zealand, and especially the Maoris, they brought the greatest gift of all, rugby.

Over the last hundred years or so the Maoris have adorned the game in New Zealand. It was and is the perfect game for them. It is a manly game, and there is no more a manly race than the Maoris. It is physically demanding, a tolerably legalised form of hand-to-hand combat. It produces a victor and a vanquished — and honour among them.

And, most important of all, it is a game of such wide expanse that there is always room for flair, for improvisation, for cocking a snook at hidebound habits. When rugby came to the Maori it offered him the perfect expression. He might have been bound by the new Pakeha laws and by English habits and customs, but he preserved his own humour, his own pride, his own slightly mischievous wish to do things slightly differently, whatever these new restrictions demanded. So rugby was the perfect vehicle for Maori expression — he loved the vigour and the rigours of it, the broad sweep of movement, the scope to laugh at the rules and rituals and to sometimes poke unorthodox fun at them.

Hika Reid, hooker, pushes through the line against French selection team.

Maori front row v.
Springboks.
Bill Bush, prop; Felix
O'Carroll, hooker; Paul
Koteka, prop.

The Welsh and the Maoris are the perfect rugby partners, and certainly this tour could not have been more perfectly timed. Over many years, but especially in the last 15 years or so, Maori rugby has passed through many moods, not all of them happy. For about 15 years after the Second World War Maori rugby flourished — an entrancing game compared with the gloomy Anglo-Saxon rugby which the All Black teams of those years produced.

But, slowly, Maori rugby fell on hard times. Some of its leaders forgot their birthright and tried to fashion Maori rugby into a Pakeha style. Others rather neglected the younger Maori players or else tried to lead them toward the path of safety first. At about the same time the sociologists and the back-room boffins began to look at the whole aspect of Maoridom and wondered, in those days of new awareness of racism, whether it was right that there should be a division between Pakeha and Maori rugby.

One of the leading Maori workers for rugby, Ralph Love, said at a New Zealand Rugby Union council meeting that he was in favour of racism in rugby if it meant the separate survival of Maori rugby. Ralph intended his remark as a throw-away quip, but it rattled a few skeletons in the cupboard. "Doc" Paewai, a noted figure in Maori rugby and education, offered the thought

Frank Shelford, flanker.

Maori All Black captain,
Bill Bush, congratulates
Errol Tobias, Springbok
fly-half, as they leave the
field at Napier after the
game ended in a draw.
Tobias was the only
coloured player in
the Springbok team.

in the 1971 Lions-Maori programme that in a modern and changing world there was not, at least in pure theory, a place for separate Maori rugby.

These were hard times for Maori rugby. New Zealand Maoris were losing matches . . . there was precious little flair, unorthodoxy or, most importantly, humour about. At the same time the New Zealand Rugby Union seemed uneasy about the future of Maori rugby.

There had been close contact with Australia, and the Australians awarded caps to their players who competed against New Zealand Maori touring teams in the decade or so after the war. But after an unhappy Maori tour in 1958 the Australians cried off. Occasionally the New Zealand Rugby Union dispatched the Maoris to Fiji, and later to Tonga and Samoa, and fielded them against major touring sides in New Zealand.

But the future was gloomy, and Maori rugby was in danger of extinction. Cometh the hour, cometh the man — or, in this case, the men. The Maoris, not always the greatest organisers in the world, decided they had to regroup. About the Auckland province, which contained a large proportion of the Maori population, the various Rugby Unions set up Maori committees, at the urging of the Maoris themselves. Soon there was a growing number of Sunday representative Maori matches amongst North Auckland, Auckland, Counties, Waikato, Thames Valley and Bay of Plenty. They fielded senior and under-21 sides. The grass-roots were starting to flourish.

And at the top appeared some notable men, past players who knew something of the pride that was the Maoris' rugby birthright. One of them was Waka Nathan, the celebrated "Black Panther", a fiery and famous loose forward with so many All Black teams of the sixties.

Gradually the two forces joined together — the new flood of Maori players from the bottom, the strong, demanding leadership from the top. By the time of the 1977 Lions tour the Maoris were almost ready. For an

Steven Pokere, centre.

hour or so they taunted and teased the Lions, bursting away to a 19-6 lead, only to have their defence crumble as the Lions escaped 22-19.

By 1979 the Maoris were ready, taking on a rigorous tour of Australia and the southern Pacific which brought an 18-all draw against the powerful Queensland side in the first match, and then six matches without defeat — including victories over New South Wales, Fiji, Western Samoa and Tonga. By now Percy Erceg, the former Auckland, North Auckland and All Black wing, had taken over from Nathan as coach, and had built on the solid foundation that Nathan had left behind.

That tour restored the Maoris' pride, and said much for their determination. Had they faltered, the tour of Wales four years hence would have wafted away like the steam from a Whakarewarewa geyser.

If there was any further proof needed that the Maoris had regained their pride and strength it came on a cold, rainy day at McLean Park, Napier, last year when the Maoris

Andy Haden playing his 100th game for New Zealand against a French Regional team.

Maori locks: Paul Tuoro
and Hud Rickit, with
Frank Shelford, flanker.

played the touring Springboks. This was the Springboks'
last rehearsal before the second Test which, after their
loss in the first Test, had to be won. The Boks were determined, very much so. And so were the Maoris. They
slashed through and around the Springbok pack, they
rattled the Springbok backs and with a few seconds to
play the Maoris led 12-9. In the last act of the game the
Springboks attacked, Colin Beck smashed a drop-kick at
the posts from close range, referee Brian Duffy, after
some hesitation, ruled it a goal, and the great victory was
snatched away from the Maoris.

Having proved themselves on the field, the Maoris
then added more cubits to their stature by accepting this
cruel trick of fate with composure, even humour. Bill
Bush, that four-square prop of so many All Black sides,
resurrected from the Canterbury scrap-heap to lead the
Maoris, was quite superb. He did not see Beck's kick, and
so could not say whether it was a goal or not. His head was
buried in the scrum. It was evidently really buried, as Bush

later said he was not too fussed about the dropped goal award for really the referee should have penalised him for deliberately collapsing the last scrum to stop the Boks' march for a push-over try.

From this resurgence of Maori rugby have come some marvellous players who, if they are not befuddled by the ruinous British winter which confounded last season's Wallabies, will light a few hearts in the valleys.

That afternoon at Napier, Frank Shelford, a wiry Bay of Plenty flanker, came from nowhere to a place in the All Black team for the third Test, and into the touring team to visit Romania and France. Shelford is the archetype Maori loose forward — lean, fast, fearless — not the cool, calculating Mourie, but a red-blooded charger after man and ball. Paul Koteka, the Waikato prop, was another dynamic man who came away from Napier looking like an All Black, which he became, winning a place on merit in the second Test against France. The Maoris at Napier found, at last, a lineout combination of the tall, lean "Hud" Rickit, the muscular power of Paul Tuoro, and the agile Jim Love towards the back.

Rickit is an interesting case, and not only because his father was so enchanted with Welsh rugby that he christened his son Haydn after Tanner — a name which somehow became the nickname of "Hud". Rickit was pitched into the first Test against Scotland early last year when Andy Haden was suspended. He jumped for 15 minutes or so, and then was seldom seen. Not the answer, said the critics, with some cause. But Rickit, a new boy lost in the Test, was a fierce and dogged competitor for the Maoris against the Springboks. It was a matter of motivation, and when Rickit is wound up no lock in New Zealand is happy marking him.

With Bush, Koteka, Hika Reid the happy hooker, Rickit, Tuoro, Love, Shelford and another fire-eating flanker Miah Melsom, the Maoris will not want for forward power and pace in Wales. To that number may well be added Paul Quinn, captain of the champion

Arthur Stone, hard-
running centre, pictured
in action against France
at Toulouse (1981).

Wellington side last year, but not available for the Maoris then. Quinn is a busy, clever forward, rather more of the Mourie mould than Shelford or Melsom.

The red-blooded vigour of the Maori forward play will be one of the strengths in Wales. If it should be joined to the artistry of their backs then a famous tour will become a great one.

And perhaps one lithe young man will lead the way. When Steven Pokere put away his soccer boots and slipped into the Southland side a few years ago the whole country rejoiced. What a player he looked . . . balanced, skilled, quick of hand and foot, and with that instinctive touch which separates the gifted from the ordinary.

Just as suddenly, Pokere was gone, like Sid Going some years before, to undertake two years' missionary work for his Mormon Church. Last year Pokere, a pleasant uncomplicated young man, came back to rugby, but slowly, for it took him time to pick up the threads, to become used again to the bumps and bruises. He did not play for the

Stu Wilson tries to get past Blanco (second Test against France).

Maoris against the Springboks, but when the call came for changes after the All Blacks lost the second Test, Pokere was in the third Test, and then went to Romania and France — once again almost lost from sight.

Like Rickit, Pokere had trouble fitting into the All Black mould, especially in a backline that never settled into any coherent pattern. But Pokere in the Maoris, should he be preserved from injury, will be another matter. The Maoris must give him his head, let him use his gifts — and by mid-November Wales may be finding a place for Pokere among their legions of midfield marvels.

The same could apply to Eddie Dunn, so brilliantly promising in 1978, but squashed out of shape in the 1979 All Blacks, who could not find a place for his flair. Dunn is

Paul Quinn, flanker, possible Maori All Black captain.

T. Wyllie, fly-half.

still a lovely player to watch and pray, heaven, his light has not been extinguished. His young brother Richard may well be the scrum-half, and he is another who needs the encouragement, the impetus of playing in a Maori side that encourages speed and spirit.

In midfield the Maoris should have two eager young men, Arthur Stone and Vic Simpson. Like Pokere, Stone was promoted to the All Blacks in Romania and France, and found the same problem of trying to fit his game into an uncomfortable All Black coat. Pokere and Stone together promise magic not possible in the All Black philosophy. Simpson is a busy and quick centre, learning the ropes. Fred Woodman, the All Black, will bring experience and speed on one wing; Robert Kururangi, now home with his Irish bride, is in the wings. So, too, is Bay of Plenty youngster John Hanley, raw but perhaps the quickest runner of them all. Warren McLean, a utility player, was full back against the Springboks, but he may not be the complete answer there, although his versatility should gain him a place in the side.

The whole of Maori rugby, and most of the rest of New Zealand, rejoiced when the New Zealand Rugby Union council decided that Waka Nathan should become manager of the Maori side. As an All Black Nathan loved Wales in 1963 and 1967 and Wales will surely love him. He is now a senior man, the Maori advisory board representative on the New Zealand Rugby Union council, but at 41 he is much the same old Waka, quick to smile, quicker to laugh, marvellously in love with rugby still. Yet he is determined that his side should perform well, that it should carry on the pride that he helped to restore to rugby in the grey days not long gone.

After his appointment Nathan made a telling point. In years gone by Maori teams would go out and play, said Nathan, and afterwards everyone would tell the Maoris what a famous game it had been. "And then," said Nathan, "they would look at the scoreboard and see they had lost. Now the Maoris play, and everyone tells them it

Eddie Dunn, fly-half for Maoris v. Springboks.

was a great game. But now the scoreboard shows a different result."

Nathan wants his Maori team to win, and I am sure the Welsh would not want it otherwise. But there was that certain twinkle in the Nathan eye as he spoke which was the surest hint that Nathan wanted to win — the Maori way. And those Welsh, with so much pride in their heritage of manly forward play and mischievous marvels in midfield, will get the chance to see the true arts of rugby. The Maoris will bring to the "haka" the kind of passion that the Welsh understand, and which the All Blacks never quite manage. They will sing with the fervour only the Welsh can comprehend. And, given luck with good weather and no injuries, the Maoris will play the kind of rugby the Welsh cherish.

How this Maori tour will lead into the kind of opposition the British Lions can expect in New Zealand next winter is more difficult to interpret. Doubtless some of the Maoris will face the Lions in the Tests — Shelford, Koteka, Reid, Stone, and hopefully Pokere. But this projection to the Lions tour next year can only be taken as a sideline to this Maori tour.

The Maoris have waited since 1926 for a tour to Europe, and Nathan's great dream has been to see New Zealand Maoris run out against the Welsh at Cardiff Arms Park. They will not be the All Blacks, nor would the Maoris want to be regarded so. They are a special, treasured and proud part of New Zealand rugby, and we envy Wales the pleasure of their company.

10
LIFE À LA REILLY

D. K. Jones

When I first started playing rugby at the secondary school, it was quickly emphasised to me by the games master that the game, being amateur, was first and foremost played to be enjoyed. This fact was indoctrinated into me at this impressionable age, and certainly from my own career it turned out to be the case. Of course, rugby in those days was not held in quite the same prominent position it enjoys in the media today, but nevertheless the game was always regarded as something of a cult in the country.

The game in Wales makes a unique contribution to the Welsh way of life, and there is no other sport which is so closely involved with the people at every level. Rugby is woven into the fabric of every Welsh community and has provoked enthusiasm that finds energetic expression in clubs and schools throughout. Like the music, language and landscape of the country, the game is a distinctive feature, and to Welshmen everywhere it is an inherent part of national prestige and pride. Rugby was always a part of my life but was never life itself, and I fully realised that if the game was played in the true amateur spirit, it could give me a lot of pleasure and enjoyment, but only for a limited period in my life.

At the age of 21 I was offered a substantial fee from the Leeds Rugby League Club to turn professional, which at the time would have been a world record transaction. The choice was not an easy one but it had to be analysed and balanced prudently. To turn professional would certainly have taken a lot of the enjoyment out of the game, but then it would have been a simple question of regarding the changeover as a total business commitment. The line of demarcation between the two different codes was a very wide one in those days, but whether this exists nowadays is a very debatable point. Anyhow, I decided that my future was with the amateur code.

I started playing for the Llanelli Rugby Club at the age of 17 and spent a most enjoyable five years with the famous "Scarlets". In my early days I was accustomed to seeing such immensely gifted players as Cyril Davies and Gareth Griffiths arriving five to ten minutes before the kick-off, quite unperturbed in the dressing room and yet always ready in time for the start. Tony O'Reilly and Andrew Mulligan would always appear during September charity games with the Gerwyn Williams XV or the Ranjii Walker XV, and one was accustomed to seeing Tony O'Reilly appearing from the opposition dressing rooms to ask whether he could borrow some wintergreen, his philosophy being that if he was not fit at this stage of the season, he had to at least smell fit. Mulligan would inevitably follow him in great humorous mood, jovial at all times, with no pre-match "butterflies" ever, but looking for some bootlaces or a towel. At Oxford University it was quite a regular feature to see I. C. Jones, the South African second row, turning up at Iffley Road carrying his kit in a pillow case. These were the typical events which I was brought up with, and which I regarded as an integral part of the amateur scene.

One of the games which I vividly remember was when both Tony O'Reilly and Andrew Mulligan appeared for the Gerwyn Williams International XV at Stradey Park. Both were late arriving, which made the secretary of the club more than slightly concerned. Obviously a large section of the crowd had come to see these two out-standing personalities in action. It so happened that it was held on a Monday, and the previous weekend they had both been with another tour — the Tankard XV — in Cornwall. It would seem that they encountered enormous difficulty in getting to the game in Llanelli in time and eventually, on the Monday afternoon, chartered a plane to Swansea Airport and from there finished the journey by taxi. Much to the relief of Arthur Davies, the secretary, they arrived in time to explain the difficulties they had had in arranging travel from Cornwall. Andrew Mulligan took the invoice for the chartered plane from his pocket as if it was a cheap day return from Bancyfelin, and presented it to Arthur, who had been patrolling constantly outside the dressing rooms, smoking cigarettes at the rate of one every 20 yards. When Mulligan commented on the amount on the invoice, Arthur looked in amazement at the piece of paper and seeing the sum involved, suddenly remarked: "Iesu Mawr, tell the President that the Club has made a take-over bid for Cambrian Airways!"

One could always appreciate the light-heartedness and the social side of the game because this was synonymous with the great characters the game seemed to be so richly endowed with. During the game itself there was always a clear objective of winning, but winning within the realms of the amateur spirit. The game was always played with great enthusiasm, determination and purpose, but if the game was lost then each man felt that he had given his best during the 80 minutes. After the final whistle, the more enjoyable, social side of the game took over without having too many ill effects. The game of rugby has never been, and will never be, a game for the faint-hearted. Any player who has had experience of playing the game in West Wales, the Midlands or the border country in Scotland will know exactly what I mean.

The strategy and tactics of the side were determined by the captain, and he was wholly responsible for the success or failure of the team. He tended to be a strong personality, demanding respect and with outstanding leadership qualities. Inevitably a team talk would take place about five minutes before the kick-off in a *tête à tête* manner, while everybody was still doing up his laces and the wintergreen was still being splashed about. Some would still be running around looking for some bandages to tie their socks up, while others would still be looking for alternative shorts to their Bermudan ones.

Peter Davies, the ex-Llanelli and Cambridge full back, recalls a lovely story while he was a student at the University. His captain at the time was Ian Beer, now headmaster of Harrow, who had gained a tremendous reputation for pre-match team talks. He would analyse and diagnose the opposition in tremendous detail, and being amongst the intellectual elite, Peter Davies had been conditioned to this. One Christmas vacation he was asked to play for Llanelli, and the captain of the side at the time was the spirited wing-forward Peter Evans — "Blondie". Apparently, five minutes before the kick-off he called for the players' attention for two minutes and, opening the programme, said, "Right lads, I guess it's every buggar for himself", and then quickly added, looking at the programme, "but No. 13 on their side is bloody mine!" That completed the team talk.

How lovely it was, during the month of September, to be involved and playing in so many charity games around the country, whether it was in Scarborough, Leicester, London or Cornwall. In fact, some of the Irish students were over here for the month because there were so many games scheduled during this time that it was completely uneconomical to be travelling back and forth to Ireland. As I have already mentioned, Llanelli always had a few of these games, and one of the personalities who frequently appeared on the wing for several seasons, and later became the darling of the Stradey crowd, was a Nigerian called Benka-Coker, who played for Richmond.

Towards the latter part of the sixties the game was taking on a new dimension, with a new professional approach and dedication. Everything was being steered in this direction without involving actual payment to the players concerned. In fact, the expectations and demands on a player nowadays are nothing short of professional standards because the amount of time the player has to devote to the game is quite considerable, particularly if he has a demanding job. This professionalism was undoubtedly established at the expense of the less serious and enjoyably moments in the game.

No doubt players nowadays are conditioned to present day standards, with the publicity and vast coverage by the media. Times change and allowance must be made for progress, and one must socially adjust to accommodate these. No doubt many players of my generation would still have displayed outstanding talent in any company, but whether they would have had so much fun and enjoyment from the game is a moot point. The game has changed enormously during the last ten years, with values and attitudes having been completely revolutionised, but this is inevitable. What changes the game has in sight during the next ten years remain to be seen, but if these are brought about with the same pace as in the last ten years then no doubt we will be talking about new and additional features in time to come. In its present context, with the price of the best seats at Twickenham at £12.00, how anyone can regard this as an amateur game mystifies me. With the development of rugby it is no wonder that the game has been restructured with new sets of ideals and a new entity. Rugby football has now become a form of commercial entertainment, but given the choice of playing as an amateur in the amateur era, or in the present format, I think with the prudence of hindsight the decision would not have been difficult to make. To me the game was meant to provide a social recreation and to be enjoyed — it was not a business.

11
A NEW ERA

David Lord

One of the most amazing selections in Australian rugby history will have an enormous impact in the future — the man is Bob Dwyer.

It has been an accepted fact throughout rugby circles that a national coach has been through "the mill". Dwyer is a different kettle of fish, surely one who rates as a punt in the big time. But don't be misled by his seemingly small experience in international rugby, his appointment was like a breath of fresh air.

Leading Randwick, the showpiece of Sydney rugby, to a first division, first grade premiership for four seasons on the trot is hardly what one could call an ideal warm-up to the biggest rugby job in the country. Somewhat an extrovert, Dwyer is without peer as a man to deploy the running game, a fact of life that for some unfathomable reason has been forgotten in the Australian rugby way of life.

The reason for such a drastic switch was the sad record of the Wallabies seventh tour of the United Kingdom, losing three out of the four internationals, only Ireland first up being a plus factor. One of the major reasons for the poor performance was the lack of running the ball from seemingly impossible positions, in short a lack of adventure. The coach on that face-losing tour was the long-standing Bob Templeton, Queenslander by birth and a man who chose to forsake what is the inherent nature of the Australian citizen: to conform to what international rugby decrees. Test rugby seems to produce safety-first rugby, akin to 10-man, 80-minute rugby, where the insurance policy is to ensure the opposition has precious little "free" ball and is therefore forced to make its own inroads into opponents . . . and as a result make mistakes of its own that allow an attack to form.

Australians aren't like that. Years of being "Colonials" in the eyes of the world, even apart from rugby, has honed an attitude that just reeks of "going it alone". The same in-bred belief applies to rugby, and once that is recognised across the board, the Wallabies will be acknowledged as top of the tree. Bob Dwyer will see to that, the man who has channelled the fortunes of Australia's greatest assets — the Ella brothers.

It would be hard for those living outside this huge continent to come to grips with the fact that a trio of Aboriginals means so much to a sport. But twins Mark and Glen, and year-younger Gary possess an indefinable something that urges crowds through the gate, in a way little different from the all-time great batsman Donald Bradman, so rightfully knighted after his services to Test cricket.

It's a long way off, but I would like to think the same accolades will fall to this marvellous trio, flag-wavers in a world where coloured sportsmen have to battle, but for this family thankfully that's not the case. Sadly, the world cannot come to grips with the divine truth that all people are born equal, that colour of skin is purely superficial. But if there's one facet of this piece on Australian rugby that says it all, then it's the simple fact that the Ellas are Australian, truly revered in every sense of the word.

As members of the all-conquering Australian Schoolboys team to the UK in 1977-78, they have come through as shining examples of what sport can provide for those fortunate to be born with outstanding ability. And that's one word that shines through Australian rugby ability. The hardest part is how to utilise that talent.

Mark Ella (Australia)
caught by Slemen and
Dodge (right).

Dwyer, having tasted outright success, and having an in-built loathing of losing, has an all-out "let's-get-up-and-at-'em" attitude to a game that lends itself to the positive thinker.

Banking on the Ellas is one thing, moulding a play pattern around players hell-bent on running is another. It may seem as though the previous comments mean the Ellas are the be-all and end-all of Australian rugby . . . far from it. While Mark weaves and bends his way through tight opposition defence with such consummate ease he almost appears bored, and Glen chimes into a backline with impeccable timing, and Gary moves in-and-away to set up supports with perfect precision, they are only three of a 15-man game.

It was a pity the three didn't fire on the UK tour, for the patrons were robbed of a sight rarely seen, inroads from nothing. But nothing should be taken away from possibly 25 other Australian players who delight in playing a 15-man game, forsaking the ever-uneventful safety first programme instituted by 99 coaches out of a 100.

Players like full back Roger Gould, a giant of a man with surprising speed, but not surprising length when boot meets ball; Brendan Moon, winger-supreme, and who must be rated one of the current-day greats with searing speed and swerve . . . and a hunger for four-pointers; Michael O'Connor, light of foot but large of pace, who performs so automatically one could be forgiven for thinking he was programmed; the unfashionable Andrew Slack, who came of age on the UK tour, consistency-plus, support-conscious, and under-rated; Michael Hawker, all class in every department; Peter Grigg, winger, paceman, defender in large doses; Mick Martin, blockbusting, fearless; Peter Carson and Phillip Cox, two half backs with only a tick between them; and three Ellas — that's a backline to make any coach's mouth water.

There are many other names that can be pencilled in for

Andy Irvine tackled by
Glen Ella during the
Hong Kong 7's.

the future, one that is assured in terms of sheer depth. David Campese, 19 years of age, a full back-cum-winger who just oozes class; Chris Stephandellis, slightly older, slightly less in ability in both positions; Damien Brown, winger of immense potential; Grant McNay and Adrian McDonald, hard-as-nails half backs, McNay an Australian schoolboy skipper against England just three years ago; Ross Hanley, another Queensland winger who thrives on being allowed room to move, and having the support inside to allow that to happen; Brad Girvan, Scott Johnson and Stephen James, adaptable to either five, eight or centre; and a host of Australian schoolboys just returned from the second undefeated tour of the UK in as many trips.

Leading that bunch is Steve Tuynman, a massively-built back rower who led that side, and in his first season out of schoolboy ranks ran headlong into the NSW side as a senior. Not far behind is Brett Papworth, slightly built but an all round centre who has already reached the national under 21 side, and can only reach higher. A 17 year-old, Matt Burke, another centre, has more years on

P. Cox gets away his pass as J. Calder tackles and the Scottish forwards bear down.

Cox passes back.

his side than most — while Michael Lynagh has already reached state status with Queensland. That's just a smattering of the talent that is available. It now becomes vital as to the way that talent is to be deployed.

In the hands of Dwyer, there can only be an upturn towards scintillating rugby that will have crowds bursting grounds at the seams. But while the back division can afford three or four sets at a top standard, there is a problem in the second row and lineout departments. Not since the days of Rob Heming, unanimously regarded as the King of Australian lineout jumpers, has there been a player to dictate prcoeedings. There have been some pretenders, some chosen piecemeal to fill berths, but none equal to the might of Heming. That gap is about to be filled with the advent of two far bigger in height than the ageless Heming. Steve Cutler and Peter FitzSimons will stamp their names into the Wallaby record books in the not-too-distant future, and stamp them as indelibly as Heming. Both are 6ft 8in, both fearless in the face of being "attended to" by the opposition, both two-handed, well controlled takers of the ball. In an era where tap ball creates so many problems, it is refreshing to see a switch to another era where giving a half back a better than even chance to clear has returned. Raw the pair may be, but all the ingredients are there for a long and highly-successful sojourn at the highest level. And for caviare, both cover with speed and solid defence to ensure their team gains maximum value from their very existence.

In the past, Australia has had to fill this vital department with extremely honest competitors such as Peter McLean, Duncan Hall, Steve Williams and Mick Mathers. Not one of them would ever give an inch, or shirk his responsibilities . . . but none was a Rob Heming, none a consistent ball-winner.

While Cutler and FitzSimons loom large, Nigel Holt — another under 21 representative — is not far behind. That augurs well for the future, especially as Australia boast back rowers of the highest calibre. Mark Loane, rated the world's top No. 8, heads the list, but as a player only. One of the most remarkable features of his play is sheer strength, and the ability to turn defence into attack. As against that, the medico cannot cope with doing his superb job as player . . . and captain as well. Perhaps that seems a savage thing to say, but it's true. Every time I have seen him shoulder the captaincy, his effectiveness on-field has been drastically reduced — and Australian rugby cannot afford such a loss.

The find of the Wallaby tour — Peter Lucas — has not only used those chances to further his rugby career, but has improved to even greater heights. As a result, rumblings are heard to move Loane into the second row, thus making room for Lucas at the back. At the time of writing there were five Tests to be played — two against Scotland and three in New Zealand — and the rumblings have yet to be answered. But there's little chance of that happening, interesting a thought as it may be on the surface.

In Simon Poidevin, the non-stop back row star of the Wallaby tour, Gary Pearse, for two seasons the victim of a string of injuries, Chris Roche, another tireless competitor who relishes the new "release-the-ball" law, Ross Reynolds, a former Country utility forward-cum-goalkicker, Jeff Miller from Queensland and his Australian under 21 flanker colleague David Maxwell from ACT and, of course, the potentially mighty Tuynman we have a band of backrowers any country would give an arm to own.

Perhaps it's a sad indictment of Australian rugby that backrowers of the highest calibre abound, whereas second

D'Arcy at work in the lineout.

rowers, props — and to a lesser extent hookers — are harder to produce. Yet maybe the day isn't far away, judging by the size of the last Australian schoolboy team to the UK — the pack was bigger overall than the Wallabies. Schoolboys around the 6ft 6ins to 6 ft 9ins mark have become common in most schools. Leaving Tony Shaw until now only emphasises his enormous worth to Australian rugby. Having lost some of his pace, yet none of his competitiveness, Shaw is a vital member of any Australian side, at home or abroad. Time has yet to prove whether those in power agree, but dropping him from the final international against England early in 1982 wasn't in anyone's interests.

Every country needs a Tony Shaw, never backward in coming forward, very much the team man. Perhaps the day will come when he moves right up front to compete against Queensland colleagues, Tony D'Arcy, Stan Pilecki, and John Meadows — the former Victorian, now a Maroon.

Down south, John Coolican, a dedicated scrummager and boasting speed off the mark that has made the odd back stretch to catch up, Sandy Muston, Ollie Hall, John Griffiths and Fred Whiteman all have little between them, but have been overshadowed by their northern cousins.

Bill Ross's return from overseas after 18 months heightens the hooker battle, with Lance Walker, the late replacement on the Wallaby tour, Bruce Malouf, the luckless one he replaced, Peter Palmer, and his under 21 competition in Wally Barnier and Tom Lawton, underlining the talent on hand.

So, that there's no denying that Australian rugby is heading for many years near the top of the international tree, with two provisos. Firstly, that rugby league makes few inroads into the top bracket, especially the younger brigade; but more importantly, that Bob Dwyer is allowed time to settle in and weave his special brand of magic, the type of game that will have spectators bursting through the gates in anticipation.

Retirements will play a part in keeping up the momentum, and quite a few players in Paul McLean, Pilecki and even Loane could follow John Hipwell and Declan Curran into that situation in the not-too-distant future. But the talent coming through is exciting, leaving Dwyer with a string of possibilities, and a series of options. With him at the helm, the green and gold of Australia, so proudly worn by the top fifteen, will be the team to beat in world rugby for many years to come.

HOME INTERNATIONALS '82

16 January, Edinburgh (Murrayfield)

SCOTLAND 9, ENGLAND 9

SCOTLAND: A. Irvine (Heriot's) *(Capt.)*; K. Robertson (Melrose); J. Renwick (Hawick); D. Johnston (Watsonians); R. Baird (Kelso); J. Rutherford (Selkirk); R. Laidlaw (Jedforest); *No. 8* I. Paxton (Selkirk); *Second Row* D. Leslie (Gala); A. Tomes (Hawick); W. Cuthbertson (Kilmarnock); J. Calder (Stewart's/Melville); *Front Row* I. Milne (Heriot's); C. Deans (Hawick); J. Aitken (Gala).

Scorers: *Penalties:* Irvine (2); *Drop Goal:* Rutherford.

ENGLAND: M. Rose (Camb. Univ.); J. Carleton (Orrell); C. Woodward, P. Dodge (Leicester); M. Slemen (Liverpool); H. Davies (Camb. Univ.); S. Smith (Sale); *No 8* R. Hesford (Bristol); *Second Row* P. Winterbottom (Headingley); M. Colclough (Angouleme); W. Beaumont (Fylde) *(Capt.)*; N. Jeavons (Moseley); *Front Row* G. Pearce (Northampton); P. Wheeler (Leicester); C. Smart (Newport).

Scorers: *Penalties:* Dodge (2), Rose.   Referee: K. Rowlands (Wales).

23 January, Dublin (Lansdowne Road)

IRELAND 20, WALES 12

IRELAND: H. MacNeill (Dublin Univ.); T. Ringland, D. Irwin (Queen's Univ.); P. Dean (St Mary's Coll.); M. Finn (Cork Const.); O. Campbell (Old Belvedere); R. McGrath (Wanderers); *No. 8* W. Duggan (Blackrock Coll.); *Second Row* J. O'Driscoll (London Irish); D. Lenihan (Univ. Coll. Cork); M. Keane (Lansdowne); F. Slattery (Blackrock Coll.); *Front Row* G. McLoughlin (Shannon); C. Fitzgerald (St Mary's Coll.) *(Capt.)*; P. Orr (Old Wesley); *Replacements:* M. Kiernan (Dolphin) for Irwin; J. Murphy (Greystones) for Dean.

Scorers: *Tries:* Ringland, Finn (2); *Conversion:* Campbell; *Penalties:* Campbell (2).

WALES: G. Evans ((Maesteg); R. Ackerman (Newport); D. Richards (Swansea); P. Daniels (Cardiff); C. Rees (London Welsh); G. Davies (Cardiff) *(Capt.)*; T. Holmes (Cardiff); *No. 8* Gareth Williams (Bridgend); R. Moriarty, G. Wheel, M. Davies (Swansea); *Front Row* G. Price (Pontypool); A. Phillips (Cardiff); I. Stephens (Bridgend). *Replacement:* G. Pearse (Bridgened) for G. Davies.

Scorers: *Try:* Holmes; *Conversion:* Evans, *Penalty:* Evans, *Drop Goal:* Pearce.

Referee: J. Short (Scotland).

6 February, London (Twickenham)

ENGLAND 15, IRELAND 16

ENGLAND: M. Rose (Cambridge Univ.); J. Carleton (Orrell); C. Woodward (Leicester); A. Bond (Sale); M. Slemen (Liverpool); H. Davies (Cambridge Univ.); S. Smith (Sale) *(Capt.)*; *No 8* J. Scott (Cardiff); *Second Row* P. Winterbottom (Headingley); M. Colclough (Angouleme); J. Syddall (Waterloo); N. Jeavons (Moseley); *Front Row* P. Blakeway (Gloucester); P. Wheeler (Leicester); C. Smart (Newport).

Scorers: *Try:* Slemen; *Conversion:* Rose; *Penalties:* Rose (3).

IRELAND: H. MacNeill (Dublin Univ.); T. Ringland (Queen's Univ.); M. Kiernan (Dolphin); P. Dean (St Mary's College); M. Finn (Cork Constitution); O. Campbell (Old Belvedere); R. McGrath (Wanderers); *No 8* W. Duggan (Blackrock College); *Second Row* J. O'Driscoll (London Irish); D. Lenihan (Univ. College Cork); M. Keane (Lansdowne); F. Slattery (Blackrock College); *Front Row* G. McLoughlin (Shannon); C. Fitzgerald (St Mary's College) *(Capt.)*; P. Orr (Old Wesley).

Scorers: *Tries:* MacNeill, McLoughlin; *Conversion:* Campbell; *Penalties:* Campbell (2).

Referee: A. Hosie (Scotland).

6 February, Cardiff (Arms Park)

WALES 22, FRANCE 12

WALES: G. Evans (Maesteg); R. A. Ackerman (Newport); D. S. Richards (Swansea); R. W. R. Gravell (Llanelli); C. F. W. Rees (London Welsh); W. G. Davies (Cardiff) *(Capt.)*; T. D. Holmes (Cardiff); *No 8* J. Squire (Pontypool); *Second Row* R. C. Burgess (Ebbw Vale); R. D. Moriarty (Swansea); S. Sutton (Pontypool); J. R. Lewis (Cardiff); *Front Row* I Stephens (Bridgend); A. J. Phillips (Cardiff); G. Price (Pontypool)

Scorers: *Try:* Holmes; *Penalties:* Evans (6).

FRANCE: M. Sallefranque (Dax); S. Blanco (Biarritz); P. Perrier (Bayonne); C. Belaiscain (Bayonne); L. Pardo (Bayonne); J. Lescarboura (Dax); G. Martinez (Toulouse); *No 8* L. Rodriguez (Mont-de-Marsan); *Second Row* J-P Rives (Toulouse) *(Capt.)*; D. Revallier (Graulhet); A. Lorieux (Grenoble); P. Lacans (Béziers); *Front Row* R. Paparemborde (Pau); P. Dintrans (Tarbes); M. Cremaschi (Lourdes).

Scorers: *Try:* Bianco; *Conversion:* Sallefranque; *Penalties:* Sallefranque, Martinez.

Referee: D. I. H. Burnett (Ireland).

20 February, Paris (Parc des Princes)

FRANCE 15, ENGLAND 27

FRANCE: M. Sallefranque (Dax); S. Blanco (Biarritz); P. Perrier, C. Belascain, L. Pardo (Bayonne); J-P. Lescarboura (Dax); G. Martine (Toulouse); *No. 8* J-L. Joinel (Brive); *Second Row* J-P. Rives (Toulouse) *(Capt.)*; M. Carpentier (Lourdes); L. Rodriguez (Mont-de-Marsan); E. Buchet (Nice); *Front Row* J-P. Wolff (Béziers); P. Dintrans (Tarbes); D. Dubroca (Agen).

Scorers: *Try:* Pardo; *Penalties:* Sallefranque (2); *Conversion:* Sallefranque; *Drop Goal:* Lescarboura.

ENGLAND: W. H. Hare (Leicester); J. Carleton (Orrell); P. W. Dodge, C. R. Woodward (Leicester); M. A. C. Slemen (Liverpool); L. Cusworth (Leicester); S. J. Smith (Sale) *Capt.)*; *No. 8* J. P. Scott (Cardiff); *Second Row* P. J. Winterbottom (Headingley); S. J. Bainbridge (Gosforth); M. J. Colclough (Angouleme); N. C. Jeavons (Moseley); *Front Row* P. J. Blakeway (Gloucester); P. J. Wheeler (Leicester); C. E. Smart (Newport).

Scorers: *Tries:* Woodward, Carleton; *Penalties:* Hare (5); *Conversions* Hare (2).

Referee: M. D. M. Rea (Ireland).

20 February, Dublin (Lansdowne Road)

IRELAND 21, SCOTLAND 12

IRELAND: H. MacNeill (Dublin Univ.); M. Finn (Cork Const.); M. Kiernan (Dolphin); P. Dean (St Mary's Coll.); K. Crossan (Instonians); O. Campbell (Old Belvedere); R. McGrath (Wanderers); *No. 8* W. Duggan (Blackrock College); *Second Row* J. O'Driscoll (London Irish); D. Lenihan (Univ. Coll. Cork); M. Keane (Lansdowne); F. Slattery (Blackrock Coll.); *Front Row* G. McLoughlin (Shannon); C. Fitzgerald (St Mary's Coll.) *(Capt.)*; P. Orr (Old Wesley).

Scorers: *Drop Goal:* Campbell; *Penalties:* Campbell (6).

SCOTLAND: A. Irvine (Heriot's) *(Capt.)*; K. Robertson (Melrose); J. Renwick (Hawick); D. Johnston (Watsonians); A. Baird (Kelso); J. Rutherford (Selkirk); R. Laidlaw (Jedforest); *No. 8* I. Paxton (Selkirk); *Second Row* E. Paxton (Kelso); A, Tomes (Hawick); J. Calder (Stewart's/Melville); *Front Row* I. Milne (Heriot's); C. Deane (Hawick); J. Aitken (Gala).

Scorers: *Try:* Rutherford; *Conversion:* Irvine; *Penalties:* Renwick (2).

Referee: C. Norling (Wales).

6 March, London (Twickenham)

ENGLAND 17, WALES 7

ENGLAND: W. Hare (Leicester); J. Carleton (Orrell); C. Woodward (Leicester); P. Dodge (Leicester); M. Slemen (Liverpool); L. Cusworth (Leicester); S. Smith (Sale) *(Capt.)*; *No. 8* J. Scott (Cardiff); *Second Row* P. Winterbottom (Headingley); M. Colclough (Angouleme); S. Bainbridge (Gosforth); N. Jeavons (Moseley); *Front Row* P. Blakeway (Gloucester); P. Wheeler (Leicester); C. Smart (Newport).

Scorers: *Tries:* Slemen, Carleton; *Penalties:* Hare (3).

WALES: G. Evans (Maesteg); R. Ackerman (Newport); R. Gravell (Llanelli); A. Donovan (Swansea); C. Rees (London Welsh); G. Davies (Cardiff) *(Capt.)*; T. Holmes (Cardiff); *No. 8* J. Squire (Pontypool); *Second Row:* R. Lewis (Cardiff); R. Moriarty (Swansea); S. Sutton (Pontypool); C. Burgess (Ebbw Vale); *Front Row* G. Price (Pontypool); A. Phillips (Cardiff); I. Stephens (Bridgend). *Replacement:* G. Williams for Homes (47 mins).

Scorers: *Try:* Lewis; *Dropped Goal:* Davies.

Referee: F. Palmade (France).

6 March Edinburgh (Murrayfield)

SCOTLAND 16, FRANCE 7

SCOTLAND: A. Irvine (Heriot's) *(Capt.)*; K. Robertson (Melrose); J. Renwick (Hawick); D. Johnston (Watsonians); G. Baird (Kelso); J. Rutherford (Selkirk); R. Laidlaw (Jedforest); *No. 8* I. Paxton (Selkirk); *Second Row* J. Calder (Stewarts/Melville); A. Tomes (Hawick); W. Cuthbertson (Kilmarnock); D. White (Gala); *Front Row* J. Aitken (Gala); C. Deans (Hawick); I. Milne (Heriot's).

Scorers: *Try:* Rutherford; *Penalties:* Irvine (3); *Dropped Goal:* Renwick.

FRANCE: M. Sallefranque (Dax); S. Blanco (Biarritz); P. Perrier (Bayonne); C. Belascain (Bayonne); L. Pardo (Bayonne); J-P Lescarboura (Dax); G. Martinez (Toulouse); *No. 8* M. Carpentier (Lourdes); *Second Row* J-P Rives (Toulouse) *(Capt.)*; L. Rodriguez (Mont-de-Marsan); D. Revallier (Graulhet); J-L Joinel (Brive); *Front Row* D. Dubroca (Agen); P. Dintrans (Tarbes); M. Cemaschi (Lourdes).

Scorers: *Try:* Rives; *Penalty:* Sallefranque.

Referee: A. Trigg (England).

20 March, Paris (Parc des Princes)

FRANCE 22, IRELAND 9

FRANCE: S. Gabernet (Toulouse); M. Fabre (Béziers); P. Mesny (Grenoble); C. Belascain (Bayonne), S. Blanco (Biarritz); J-P. Lescarboura (Dax); P. Berbizier (Lourdes); *No. 8* J-L Joinel (Brive); *Second Row* L. Rodriguez (Mont-de-Marsan); J-F Imbernon (Perpignon); D. Revallier (Graulhet); J-P Rives (Toulouse) *(Capt.)*; *Front Row* R. Paparemborde (Pau); P. Dintrans (Tarbes); P. Dospital (Bayonne). *Replacement:* P. Perrier (Bayonne) for Belascain (60 mins).

Scorers: *Tries* Blanco, Mesny; *Conversion:* Gabernet; *Penalties:* Blanco (2), Gabernet (2).

IRELAND: H. MacNeill (Dublin Univ.); T. Ringland (Queen's Univ.); M. Kiernan (Dolphine); P. Dean (St Mary's Coll.); M. Finn (Cork Constitution); O. Campbell (Old Belvedere); R. McGrath (Wanderers); *No. 8* J. O'Driscoll (London Irish); *Second Row* R. Kearney (Wanderers); D. Lenihan (Univ. Coll. Cork); M. Keane (Lansdowne); F. Slattery (Blackrock Coll.); *Front Row* G. McLoughlin (Shannon); C. Fitzgerald (St Mary's Coll.) *(Capt.);* P. Orr (Old Wesley).

Scorers: *Penalties:* Campbell (3)

Referee: A. Welsby (England)

20 March, Cardiff (Arms Park)

WALES 18, SCOTLAND 24

WALES: G. Evans (Maesteg); R. Ackerman (Newport); R. Gravell (Llanelli); A. Donovan (Swansea); C. Rees (London Welsh); G. Davies (Cardiff) *(Capt.);* G. Williams (Bridgend); *No 8* E. Butler (Pontypool); *Second Row* R. Lewis (Cardiff); R. Moriarty (Swansea); R. Norster (Cardiff); C. Burgess (Ebbw Vale); *Front Row* G. Price (Pontypool); A. Phillips (Cardiff); I. Stephens (Bridgend).

Scorers: *Try:* Butler; *Conversion:* Evans. *Penalties:* Evans (4).

SCOTLAND: A. Irvine (Heriot's) *(Capt.)*; J. Pollock (Gosforth); J. Renwick (Hawick); D. Johnston (Watsonians); G. Baird (Kelso); J. Rutherford (Selkirk); R. Laidlaw (Jedforest); *No. 8* I. Paxton (Selkirk); *Second Row* D. White (Gala); A. Tomes (Hawick); W. Cuthbertson (Kilmarnock); J. Calder (Stewarts-Melville); *Front Row* I. Milne (Heriot's); C. Beans (Hawick); J. Aitken (Gala). *Replacement:* G. Dickson for Paxton (15 mins)

Scorers: *Tries:* Calder, Renwick, Pollock, White, Johnston; *Conversions:* Irvine (4); *Dropped Goals:* Renwick, Rutherford.

Referee: J-P. Bonnet (France).

OVERSEAS TOURS

New Zealand tour of France, 20 October - 21 November, 1981

TOUR DETAILS

Venue	Opponents	Result
Constanta, 20 Oct.	Southern Romania XV	25-9 (NZ)
Bucharest, 24 Oct.	Romania	14-6 (NZ)
Strasbourg, 28 Oct.	French Selection	15-13 (NZ)
Clermont-Ferrand, 31 Oct.	French Selection	18-10 (NZ)
Grenoble, 4 Nov.	French Selection	16-18 (F)
Bayonne, 7 Nov.	French Barbarians	28-18 (NZ)
Perpignan, 11 Nov.	French Selection	6-6
Toulouse, 14 Nov.	FRANCE	13-9 (NZ)
La Rochelle, 17 Nov.	French Selection	17-13 (NZ)
Paris, 21 Nov.	FRANCE	18-6 (NZ)

14 November, Toulouse

FRANCE 9 (2PG IDG)   New Zealand 13 (2PG IDG IT)

FRANCE: S. Gabernet (Toulouse); M. Fabre (Béziers); R. Bertranne (Bagnères); P. Mesny (Grenoble); S. Blanco (Biarritz); G. Laporte (Graulhet); P. Berbizier (Lourdes); *No. 8* D. Erbani (Agen); *Second Row* J-L Joinel (Brive); A. Lorieux (Grenoble); D. Revallier (Graulhet); L. Rodriguez (Mont-de-Marsan); *Front Row:* R. Paparemborde (Pau) (*Capt.*); P. Dintrans (Tarbes); M. Cremaschi (Lourdes).

Scorers: *Penalty Goals:* Laporte (2); *Dropped Goal:* Gabernet

NEW ZEALAND: Hewson; Wilson; Salmon; Stone; Fraser; McKechnie; Loveridge; *No. 8* Mexted; *Second Row* Mourie (*Capt.*); Haden; Whetton; Shaw; *Front Row:* Spiers; Dalton; Ketels. *Replacement:* Rollerson for McKechnie (59 mins).

Scorers: *Try:* Wilson; *Penalty Goals:* Hewson (2); *Dropped Goal:* Hewson

Referee: C. Norling (Wales). Attendance 15,000

21 November, Paris (Parc des Princes)

FRANCE 6 (2PG)   NEW ZEALAND 18 (2G 2PG)

FRANCE: S. Gabernet (Toulouse); M. Fabre (Béziers); R. Betranne (Bagnères); P. Mesny (Grenoble); S. Blanco (Biarritz); G. Laporte (Graùlhet); P. Berbizier (Lourdes); *No. 8:* D. Erbani (Agen); *Second Row:* J. L. Joinel (Brive); A. Lorieux (Grenoble); D. Revallier (Graulhet); L. Rodriguez (Mont-de-Marsan); *Front Row:* R. Paparemborde (Pau) (*Capt.*); P. Dintrans (Tarbes); M. Cremaschi (Lourdes); *Replacement:* D. Dubroca (Agen) for Crémaschi (29 mins).

Scorers: *Penalty Goals:* Laporte, Blanco

NEW ZEALAND: Hewson; Fraser; Wilson; Stone; Woodman; Rollerson; Loveridge; *No. 8:* Mexted; *Second Row:* Mourie (*Capt.*); Haden; Whetton; Shaw; *Front Row:* Spiers; Dalton; Koteka; *Replacement:* Salmon for Fraser (6 mins).

Scorers: *Tries:* Shaw (pen.); Wilson; *Conversions:* Hewson (2); *Penalty Goals:* Hewson (2)

Referee: J. R. West (Ireland).   Attendance 34,000

Information by courtesy of Rothmans Publications Limited

England tour of North America, 24 May - 19 June 1982

TOUR DETAILS

Venue	*Opponents*	*Result*
Toronto, 24 May	Eastern Canada	52-3 (E)
Vancouver, 29 May	CANADA	43-6 (E)
Bothell, Seattle, 3 June	US Cougars	26-6 (E)
Long Beach, 5 June	Pacific Coast	28-6 (E)
Dallas, Texas, 9 June	Western Rugby Union	45-6 (E)
Cleveland, 13 June	Mid-West	58-9 (E)
New York, 16 June	Eastern Rugby Union	41-0 (E)
Hartford, Connecticut, 19 June	USA	59-0 (E)

ENGLAND

Smith (*Capt.*), Carleton, McDowell, Swift, Colclough, Woodward, Stringer, Cusworth, Jeavons, Scott, Gadd, Rendall, Wheeler, Bainbridge, Hare, Blakeway, Winterbottom.

Overall Result:

8 victories, 53 tries, 352 points

Scotland tour of Australia, 10 June - 10 July, 1982

TOUR DETAILS

Venue	Opponents	Result
Brisbane, 10 June	Queensland County XV	44-16 (S)
Brisbane, 13 June	Queensland	18-7 (A)
Sydney, 19 June	Sydney	22-13 (A)
Melbourne, 23 June	Victoria XV	38-3 (S)
Sydney, 26 June	New South Wales	31-7 (S)
Singleton, 29 June	New South Wales Country XV	44-3 (S)
Brisbane, 4 July	AUSTRALIA	12-7 (S)
Canberra, 6 July	Australian Capital Territory	22-4 (S)
Sydney, 10 July	AUSTRALIA	33-9 (A)

SCOTLAND

Irvine (*Capt.*), Baird, Johnston, Gordon, Robertson, Rutherford, Laidlaw, Milne, Deans, McGuinness, Tomes, Cuthbertson, Paxton, Calder, White, Williamson, Aitken, Dods, Pollock, Hunter, Cunningham, Rowan, McKie.

Hong Kong: the home of World 7s.

Information by courtesy of the Daily Telegraph Library.